A SERIES OF LESSONS IN ISLAM

Creed

GOD AND HIS AMBASSADORS

Sayyid Ali Al-Hakeem

THE MAINSTAY
FOUNDATION

Author: Sayyid Ali Al-Hakeem

Translated and Edited by: The Mainstay Foundation

© 2015 The Mainstay Foundation

Printed in the United States.

ISBN: 978-1943393930

To our guide. To our hope. To our salvation.

To our Prophet (s).

CONTENTS

ABOUT THE AUTHOR

Sayyid Ali Al-Hakeem is an esteemed Muslim scholar, lecturer, and researcher residing in Dubai, UAE. Sayyid Al-Hakeem spent ten years studying at the Islamic seminaries of Qum, Iran. There, he completed his Advanced Seminars (a Ph.D. equivalent in Islamic seminaries) in Islamic Jurisprudence and Thought. He also received a Master's degree in Islamic Thought from the Islamic University of Lebanon. Sayyid Al-Hakeem has dedicated the past twenty-two years of his life to service of the Muslim community in different capacities. He serves as a resident scholar in the Imam Hassan Mosque, Dubai. He is the Chair of the Religious Committee and the religious supervisor of the Charitable Deeds Committee of the Ja'afariya Endowment Charitable Council of Dubai.

TRANSLATOR'S PREFACE

The task of translating Sayyid Ali Al-Hakeem's book was gratifying and enlightening. The book delivered precious nuggets of knowledge and polished pearls of wisdom in a style that is conversational and pleasant. This book is our attempt to pass these nuggets and pearls on to you in a style that is similarly conversational and pleasant. We thank the Sayyid for allowing us to benefit from this endeavor. We wish for him a life filled with scholarly attainment, in hopes that he will continue to pass along his treasures.

Here, we must humbly admit some of our biggest limitations. First, we must admit the great difficulty that comes with the attempting to translate the Holy Quran. Muslim scholars have pondered on the meanings of the holy text for centuries, and the meanings of its verses only grow deeper as time passes. The process of translation always begs us to find precise meanings for the passages that we translate. But when we encounter the majesty of the Holy Quran, we find ourselves incapable of understanding, let alone translating, its true and deep meanings. We turned to the works of translators who have attempted to do this before. Although no translation can do justice to the Holy Quran, we found that the translation of Ali Quri Qarai to be the most proper in understanding when compared to the understanding of the text as derived by our grand scholars. As such, we decided to rely on Qarai's translations throughout this book, with some adaptations that allowed us to weave the verses more properly with the rest of the work.

A second great limitation came with translation of the narrations of the Grand Prophet Muhammad (s) and his Holy Household (a). Their words are ever so deep and ever so powerful. We attempted to convey these passages to the reader in a tone that is understandable without deviating from the essence of the words of these immaculate personalities. We pray that we were successful in this endeavor.

Finally, we want to take this opportunity to thank you for your support. As students of Islam and as translators of this text, our greatest purpose is to please God by passing along these teachings to others. By picking up this book, you have lent your crucial support in this endeavor. We hope that you will continue your support throughout the rest of this book, and we ask that you keep us in prayers whenever you pick it up.

The Editorial and Translation Team,
The Mainstay Foundation

INTRODUCTION

In the name of God, the most Beneficent, the most Merciful

Praise be to God, Lord of the Worlds. May God send His peace and blessings to the most noble of His creatures, the Holy Prophet Muhammad (s) and his Progeny (a).

This book, *Creed: God and His Ambassadors*, is a compilation of lessons in creed revolving around specific discussions on our relationship with God and His representatives (i.e. prophets, messengers, imams). It addresses a number of topics that are key to the Shia Muslim world-view. Emphasis is given, first and foremost, to our relationship with the Creator. The book then addresses the message and example of our Grand Prophet (s) and his Holy Household. The book concludes with a brief chapter on death as our transition to the afterlife.

The teachings of Islam have one unequivocal goal – to allow its followers to pursue excellence. From that perspective, Islam places great emphasis on knowledge and learning. We can see this clearly in the verses of the Holy Quran. These verses give knowledge a special status that is unique when compared with other human virtues. God says in the

Holy Quran, "*Say, 'Are those who know equal to those who do not know?' Only those who possess intellect take admonition.*"[1] God also says, "*Only those of God's servants having knowledge fear Him.*"[2]

The traditions of the Holy Prophet (s) and his Progeny (a) contain numerous similar admonitions as well. It is narrated that Imam Al-Sadiq (a) said, "*The Messenger of God (s) once said, 'Seeking knowledge is an obligation on every Muslim. Verily, God loves the seekers of knowledge.*" It is also narrated that the Commander of the Faithful Ali ibn Abi Talib (a) once said,

> *Oh people! Know that excellence in faith consists of seeking knowledge and acting in accordance to that knowledge. Indeed, seeking knowledge is a higher obligation for you than seeking sustenance. Your sustenance is pre-ordained and guaranteed. Your Just Lord has divided it amongst you and promised to deliver it to you. Surely, He will keep His promise. [On the other hand,] knowledge is protected by its keepers. You were commanded to seek it from its keepers, so go forth and seek it.*

Islam did not stop at admonitions and theories about knowledge and learning. Instead, it created opportunities and enabled conditions that would foster learning, research, and study. Amongst these was the establishment of Friday prayers – God says in the Quran, "*O you who have faith! When the call is made for prayer on Friday, hurry toward the remembrance of God, and leave all business. That is better for you, should you know.*"[3] One of the important pillars of this ritual is its sermon, where the prayer leader must convey Islam's teachings, in

---

[1] The Holy Quran. Chapter 39 [Arabic: *Al-Zumar*]. Verse 9.

[2] The Holy Quran. Chapter 35 [Arabic: *Fatir*]. Verse 28.

[3] The Holy Quran. Chapter 62 [Friday; Arabic: *Al-Jumaa*]. Verse 9.

addition to addressing all other relevant worldly and other-worldly matters.

Dear reader, this series of books is based on a compilation of Friday sermons that I delivered over the years, as well as lectures I gave at a number of commemorations and celebrations. Throughout such gatherings, I have been able to address and speak on a wide array of issues relevant to the Muslim community.

At the insistence of a number of dear brothers, I compiled my notes to write these books with the hopes that God will accept the work and that the benefit will spread to the believers. I tried to maintain the conversational tone of the original sermons in order to make the books more reader friendly. After a series of these books were printed in the original Arabic, a group of believers then insisted to have the work translated into English so that English-speaking audiences may benefit as well.

I thank God, the Exalted, for His infinite support and favor. I must also thank everyone who participated in making this book a reality.

I ask God, the Almighty, to take this work as an act of devotion for His sake and to accept it by His grace, He is surely the All-Kind and Magnanimous.

Ali Al-Hakeem,
Dubai, United Arab Emirates

WHY STUDY CREED?

In the Name of God, the most Beneficent, the most Merciful

Alif Lam Mim. This is the Book, there is no doubt in it, a guidance to the Godwary, who believe in the Unseen, maintain the prayer, and spend out of what We have provided for them; and who believe in what has been sent down to you and what was sent down before you, and are certain of the Hereafter. Those follow their Lord's guidance and it is they who are the felicitous.[1]

God created humans and cared for them greatly, which is suitable given the robust potential and abilities God has bestowed on mankind. Humans are distinguished among all of God's creation in their intellect and free will. therefore,it is only natural that God's divine care would encompass mankind in all its kindness and generosity, in a way that is distinct from the rest of creation because humanity is distinct from the rest of creation. The greatest distinction was sending divine messages that led people out of the darkness of ignorance to the light of knowledge and comprehension. God said, "*Alif, Lam, Ra. [This is] a Book We have sent down to*

---

[1] The Holy Quran. Chapter 2 [The Cow; Arabic: *Al-Baqara*]. Verse 1-5.

you that you may bring mankind out from darkness into light, by the command of their Lord, to the path of the All-mighty, the All-laudable."[2]

Many however, did not care for this divine provision, they did not work to benefit from the Books of Heaven, nor did they utilize the intellect which God distinguished them with. Instead of striving for their excellence and happiness, which is only realized through knowledge of God, they yearned for this world and its fading enjoyments.

In addition, there are people who do not exert even the minimal effort in thinking and reflection that is the key to realizing one's excellence. Thus, such people will live in a state of confusion throughout their lives. A person of this sort does not know how to conduct himself because he has not learned the essential matters that will allow him to realize happiness. Such a person settled for building his entire religion on simply following in the footsteps of his forefathers, without engaging his intellect by reasoning and reflection.

God addresses the shameful state of such people in the Holy Quran with the following verse: *"Indeed the worst of beasts in God's sight are the deaf and dumb who do not exercise their reason."*[3]

> *Certainly We have winnowed out for hell many of the jinn and humans: they have hearts with which they do not understand, they have eyes with which they do not see, they have*

---

[2] The Holy Quran. Chapter 14 [Arabic: *Ibrahim*]. Verse 1.
[3] The Holy Quran. Chapter 8 [The Spoils of War; Arabic: *Al-Anfaal*]. Verse 22.

ears with which they do not hear. They are like cattle; in-deed, they are more astray. It is they who are the heedless.[4]

Humans are expected to utilize their intellect in order to attain religious knowledge and awareness that will bring one towards excellence. God points to this in the following verse: *"I did not create the jinn and the humans except that they may worship Me."*[5] The service and worship of God is an instrument to reaching one's greatness which is attached to certainty in God. Through worshipping God Almighty, humans can achieve greater levels of excellence until death befalls them. *"And worship your Lord until certainty comes to you."*[6] Our excellence as human beings comes as a result of our of knowledge and certainty in God. This cannot be achieved without hard work and dedication. In light of this realization, we can delve into the following points:

WHAT MUST BE STUDIED?

Religious knowledge can be divided into two categories:

The first category is knowledge that is linked to God Almighty, His Oneness and the Resurrection, Furthermore, this category relates to the attributes of God, Divinely appointed leadership (i.e. prophets and imams), His messengers, the divine messages, and the Books of God.

The second category is knowledge related to the laws and regulations for social etiquette and individual practice ranging from worship to transactions. Through our relationship

---

[4] The Holy Quran. Chapter 7 [The Heights; Arabic: *Al-Araf*]. Verse 179.

[5] The Holy Quran. Chapter 51 [Arabic: *Al-Dhariyat*]. Verse 56.

[6] The Holy Quran. Chapter 15 [Arabic: *Al-Hijr*]. Verse 99.

with God, we are bound to develop etiquettes in interacting with our fellow man. This applies to both our ethics in relationships , business and cultural transactions.

Both of these categories of knowledge are derived from certain rational reasoning, the Divine revelation and the traditions of the immaculate Prophet (s). One cannot utilize this knowledge and adhere to it unless he has the proper proofs and evidence to lead him in the right direction.

There is a difference between the two categories . The first category relates to the specific knowledge and firm faith one must have regarding religion; thus, we describe this category as creed. Creed involves the principles of belief that the heart latches on to, which must be rooted in certainty. Thus, we observe that our religion does not permit us to do *taqleed* (emulate a qualified jurist) in the matters of *tawheed* (oneness of God), *nubuwwa* (prophethood), *imamate* (divinely appointed leaders), nor *ma'aad* (resurrection). This would not make sense, as belief in something with one's heart is different than simply following someone else's opinion in practice. Rather, we, as individuals, must have beliefs rooted in certainty, even if it is only at the most basic level. Believing in the oneness of God, His perfect attributes and having faith in His message, His Books, and especially His prophets, messengers, and imams, and the Day of Judgment – these are all principles that we must have our own conviction about and not simply follow or emulate the opinion of a jurist or individual without our own conviction rooted in certainty.

The second category does not require us to have belief and knowledge of its specificities; it is enough for a person to do *taqleed* (emulate a qualified jurist) in these matters. These are opinions to be followed in practice, and do not require one to have a personal conviction regarding the evidence behind them. In these matters, it is enough to follow the conclusions of the qualified jurist in practice. Thus, the first category is described as *usool al-deen* (the principles of religion), because it forms the fundamental principles that our religion is based on. The second category, is described as *furoo' al-deen* (the branches of religion).

In regards to *furoo' al-deen*, a person is free to seek the knowledge by becoming a qualified jurist himself, which is a tremendous task and is not practically possible for everyone, or perform *taqleed*. In doing *taqleed*, you are emulating or referring back to the experts of this area of knowledge in regards to its laws in both worship and transactions. These experts are our Islamic jurists, may God protect and reward them.

There are, however two fundamental problems in the way people deal with this area of study. One being that many people don't give this area much importance, which is not only upsetting but extremely dangerous in both this life and the next as the status of man in the afterlife is built around this knowledge .God points to this problem in the following verse: *"Yet most people will not have faith, however eager you should be."*[7] Some just continue doing what they found their forefathers doing: *"No, they said, 'We found our fathers following a creed, and we are indeed guided in their footsteps.'"*[8]

---

[7] The Holy Quran. Chapter 12 [Arabic: *Yusuf*]. Verse 103.
[8] The Holy Quran. Chapter 43 [Arabic: *Al-Zukhruf*]. Verse 22.

From this point, we can observe the problem of polytheism and atheism. From such perspective , many people do not care enough to want to know and thus do not try to seek out true happiness. Rather, such individuals may convince themselves that they already have the truth, therefore they defend their false beliefs blindly. Extremism can play a motivating factor, for it pushes such a person to defend beliefs that are clearly misguided simply because they were the beliefs of this person's forefathers.

On the other hand, there are those who do care about these issues. They seek out this knowledge in creed, but they do not reach the truth due to taking an incorrect approach to seeking knowledge. Intellectual research must be built on the foundation of logic and reason in order to reach the correct conclusions. To depend on non-scientific or non-intellectual methods will undoubtedly deliver uncertain results and conclusions. Hence, utilizing incorrect methods will result in reaching wrong conclusions while thinking one is correct in his belief or creed. Having the correct creed is the foundation for a person's journey on the road to God. *"Say, 'This is my way. I summon to God with insight – I and he who follows me. Immaculate is God, and I am not one of the polytheists.'"*[9]

THE DIFFICULTY OF RELIGIOUS LEARNING

People often give excuses as to why they cannot study theology or creed to deepen their understanding, the most common excuse being that the terminology used is confusing or not easy to understand. Another excuse is that there

[9] The Holy Quran. Chapter 12 [Arabic: *Yusuf*]. Verse 108.

are so many different schools of thought out there with their own perspective and proofs that it is not clear what position is the correct one.

Let us discuss a few points and address these problematic propositions:

The fact that there are various opinions and difference in outlook is not incompatible with the reality that the truth is still clear. If a person sincerely wants to seek truth and does so by intellectual and logical means, he will reach it. Or, at least, the person will be excused for trying his very best. But one is not excused when he knowingly fails to utilize the correct tools and methods or chooses to accumulate a background that further conceals him from the truth. These backgrounds could be financial interests that sway his perspective, or a blind attachment to what he holds on to in faith. Such a person is not excused before God, because he did not transcend these backgrounds, which held him back from reaching the truth.

God created religion and ordained it for mankind. Such a religion must be clear so that people acknowledge and follow it. Otherwise, their responsibility to follow such a religion would be one that cannot be realized. Knowledge of creed, no matter how simple it may be to realize through the intellectual means, can be realized by one's unadulterated innate nature. The same faculties that allow an individual to differentiate between right and wrong, just and unjust, even if it is at the most basic level, allow one to reach truth in the knowledge of creed.

In addition, it is not required from every individual to independently utilize and depend on the specific scientific tools and intricate intellectual inferences that do not come naturally for everyone in the knowledge of creed. These tools are indeed used by those who delve deep into the study of theology and creed. What is required of each individual, however, is to have faith based on reason, even if it is at the most basic level. The emphasis here is that the faith must be built on the foundations of knowledge and proper premise in reasoning.

The more one studies and deepens his research in the matters of theology, the greater his awareness and knowledge of the creed will be. Such a person will be at a higher and better state than others if he upholds that awareness in his life. This does not infer that the others are excused from studying; rather, one should not shortchange himself from reaching certainty in their knowledge of creed. But the level of knowledge will differ from one who is an expert dedicated to studies versus a layperson who is not. Take one's health for example. Everyone should take care of their bodies and ensure that they are healthy. Everyone is capable of ensuring their physical health. There are, however, individuals that specialize in this area and focus their time studying the methods of ensuring a healthy lifestyle. Such a person is naturally going to have more knowledge, information, and general know-how in this area due to the time they invested in studying it. Rarely, however does one find an individual (who is not a medical professional) that is unable to maintain his health. This reality applies in the same way when it comes to theology and the study of creed – individual capacity levels differ, but every individual is expected to perform and has a responsibility to do so.

Furthermore, the difficulty of seeking knowledge does not excuse a person from doing so. A person must seek out this knowledge because it determines one's true success in this life and the next. Knowledge that affects so many aspects of our life – our lifestyle, our comfort, and our happiness – should be a high priority for us. Difficulty should not be an excuse to abandon the search; it should be motivation to make a worthy achievement.

THE IMPORTANCE OF CREED

There are a number of reasons for why studying creed is so essential. The state and condition of our afterlife, i.e. reward and punishment, is subject to our knowledge in creed and the level of faith we have in it. It is true that we are judged based on the *furoo'*, our practices, but the *furoo'* do not equate in importance to the knowledge of creed. Notice that when a person dies and is buried, it is recommended to remind the soul of fundamental elements of creed. This indicates that creed is so essential that reminding the soul of its elements helps one in his or her transition from this life to the next. Even on the Day of Judgment, we will all stand and be questioned about our actions, including actions of the heart (our beliefs). What was our reason for that belief? If we are not justified and excused, the wrongdoers amongst us may hopelessly try to make up excuses, but to no avail: *"The day [will come] when every soul will come pleading for itself and every soul will be recompensed fully for what it has done, and they will not be wronged."*[10]

---

[10] The Holy Quran. Chapter 16 [The Bees; Arabic: *Al-Nahl*]. Verse 111.

The emphasis on creed and usool al-deen does not mean that the furoo' and an individuals' deeds are not significant as well. However , creed forms the foundation of that significance, because if a person dies with the correct creed then he will be encompassed by the mercy of God by way of intercession, forgiveness and pardon. However, if a person dies with a creed outside of monotheism, and without any justification such as insanity or any other valid excuse for holding that belief, then his deeds will not save him. The value and effect of our deeds are contingent on the soundness of our creed.

> *Those who do not expect to encounter Us say, 'Why have angels not been sent down to us, or why do we not see our Lord?' Certainly, they are full of arrogance within their souls and have become terribly defiant. The day they will see the angels, there will be no good news for the guilty on that day, and they will say, 'Keep off [from paradise]!' Then We shall attend to the works they have done and then turn them into scattered dust.*[11]

Correcting one's worship and social conduct based on sound creed is essential. Our creed directly reflects how we conduct ourselves. The more sound the creed, the greater effect it will have on our actions and conduct, as demonstrated by the following examples.

The belief in free will and the lack of free will have a direct influence on the conduct and demeanor of the individual, both socially and in worship. Believing that our actions are forced and we have no control over our fate changes the

---

[11] The Holy Quran. Chapter 25 [Arabic: *Al-Furqan*]. Verses 21-23.

way a person looks at his actions especially in regards to responsibility and accountability. When you counter this with the creed of free will, you also observe the distinction in conduct and demeanor. A person that believes in free will acknowledges that he has a decision and is responsible for his choices. His free will falls within the scope of God's will, but nonetheless, the individual has the freedom to choose and is judged based on his choice. These two beliefs differ completely from one another and their reflection on a person's lifestyle is very different. The former creed puts everything on God, removing any responsibility from the individual and lessening any feeling of remorse or guilt for bad deeds. The latter, on the other hand, claims responsibility within the scope of God's will, thus changing the person's outlook and dealings with those around him.

The belief in the Holy Prophet's (s) and Ahlulbayt's (a) continuing presence in our lives even after their death is another essential belief. Your relationship, the way you interact and feel about the Prophet (s) and the Ahlulbayt (a) differs completely based on this belief. They see our deeds and are witness to them, as evidenced by the Holy Quran: "*And say, 'Go on working: God will see your conduct, and His Apostle and the faithful [as well], and you will be returned to the Knower of the sensible and the Unseen, and He will inform you concerning what you used to do.*"[12] In another verse God says, "*Thus We have made you a middle nation that you may be witnesses to the people, and that the Apostle may be a witness to you...*"[13]

---

[12] The Holy Quran. Chapter 9 [The Repentance; Arabic: *Al-Tawba*]. Verse 105.
[13] The Holy Quran. Chapter 2 [The Cow; Arabic: *Al-Baqara*]. Verse 143.

For the person that believes that the extent of the Prophet's (s) status is limited to before his death, that person does not interact with the Prophet in beseeching him and praying to God through his intercession. This is unlike individuals who believe in the Prophet's (s) and Ahlulbayt's (a) influence and status beyond their death, who appeal to God through them and ask for their intercession in fulfilling their needs and desires.

Furthermore, the belief in imamate and the authority of Ahlulbayt (a) is also fundamental. Those who have this belief see their words, verdicts, and actions as a religious proof just like that of the Holy Prophet (s). Lack of such a belief naturally does not attribute that legislative value. They are in turn looked at like any other narrator of the Prophet's (s) tradition, with no special status compared to the others that came after the Holy Prophet (s).

Knowledge of creed has a large role in the completion of one's ideology and system of thought. Through one's creed the big picture of questions regarding our existence, our purpose, the origin of the universe, where it is going and why, become clearer. The more we know within the study of creed and theology, the better we understand the world around us.

The Divine Trust

In the Name of God, the most Beneficent, the most Merciful

Indeed We presented the Trust to the heavens and the earth and the mountains, but they refused to undertake it and were apprehensive of it; but man undertook it. Indeed he is most unjust and ignorant.[1]

Man's Abilities

When we reflect on the creations of God, we see that some of them are majestic, expansive, and strong, such as this universe that has baffled man for so many millennia. The Earth that is so small compared to other cosmic bodies, but is so large and majestic in our eyes. The mountains that make us look so inconsequential compared to their size and strength. When we reflect on our own condition and the influence of our natural desires on us, we find that we are weak. The Quran testifies to this truth in the verse *"God desires to lighten your burden, for man was created weak."*[2] Moreover,

---

[1] The Holy Quran. Chapter 33 [The Factions; Arabic: *Al-Ahzab*]. Verse 72.
[2] The Holy Quran. Chapter 4 [The Women; Arabic: *Al-Nisaa*]. Verse 28.

we see that mankind stands powerless at times, even against the puniest of creations.

> *O people! Listen to a parable that is being drawn: Indeed those whom you invoke besides God will never create [even] a fly even if they all rallied to do so! And if a fly should take away something from them, they cannot recover that from it. Feeble is the seeker and the sought!*[3]

But despite this feeble creation that we have been granted, God has blessed us with a number of abilities that allow us to control our surroundings and benefit from other creatures. These abilities include the intellect, the will, and determination. Mankind uses these abilities to strive towards anything that he desires. If his body is not powerful enough to do something, he will use his ingenuity and will to get what he wants. In that sense, we are one of the highest and most majestical of creations.

This is the difference between mankind and all other creations that may appear more powerful and majestic, but that have become tools in our hands. Here, we understand the meaning of the verse, *"It is God who disposed the sea for you[r benefit] so that the ships may sail in it by His command, that you may seek of His bounty and that you may give thanks. He has disposed for you[r benefit] whatever is in the heavens and whatever is on the earth; all is from Him. There are indeed signs in that for a people who reflect."*[4] Everything in this world is at the disposal of our intellects and our will.

---

[3] The Holy Quran. Chapter 22 [The Pilgrimage; Arabic: *Al-Hajj*]. Verse 73.

[4] The Holy Quran. Chapter 45 [Arabic: *Al-Jathiya*]. Verses 12, 13.

THE RECKONING

God did not create this universe without a purpose for the creatures to achieve. In every single aspect of creation, God has a plan and a wisdom. God Almighty, who has no needs or deficiencies, is surely beyond frivolous or even mediocre choices. As the Quran articulates, *"We did not create the sky and the earth and whatever is between them for play. Had We desired to take up some diversion We would have taken it up with Ourselves, were We to do [so]."*[5]

Because we know that God's act of creation is not frivolous, we know that there must be some type of reckoning for that which takes place in the universe. Part of that which occurs in the universe is the act of free will demonstated by humans. Free will entails responsibility; if the exercise of free will is not accounted for somehow, either through some form of reward for good deeds or punishment for bad deeds, then the creation of free willed beings would be pointless. The lack of accountability would mean futility and frivolousness in creation. The greater that a being is, the greater the responsibility it bears. God draws our attention to this connection between the serious, non-frivolous nature of creation and between reckoning and judgment in the following verse: *"Did you suppose that We created you aimlessly, and that you will not be brought back to Us?"*[6]

The verse clearly indicates that there will be a return to God and that there will be a judgment on all our actions and be-

---

[5] The Holy Quran. Chapter 21 [The Prophets; Arabic: *Al-Anbiya*]. Verses 16, 17.

[6] The Holy Quran. Chapter 23 [The Believers; Arabic: *Al-Mu'minoon*]. Verse 115.

haviors. Because God's act of creation was full of wisdom, there must be responsibility and judgment for all actions.

Not only is God's creation purposeful with great goals. Moreover, God has also set mankind at the center of the divine purpose, in light of the great deal of abilities that we have been granted in spite of our feeble bodies. This is why mankind was the carrier of God's great trust.

What is this trust? How was it given to mankind? Was mankind able to bear it? What is the role of this trust in our lives?

THE DIVINE TRUST

Interpreters of the Holy Quran differ on the meaning of the "trust" that God gave to mankind. The following is a list of some of the most important interpretations:

1. Some scholars interpreted the trust as "divine agency and the highest levels of servitude and worship that can be reached through knowledge and good deeds."

2. Other scholars interpreted it as "freedom of choice and will that distinguish humanity from all other creations."

3. Another interpretation claims that it is "the intellect that is the recipient of divine commands and the faculty by which a person deserves reward or punishment."

4. The trust has also been interpreted as "the limbs of the human body. So, for example, the eye is a trust and must be safeguarded so that it is not used in

disobedience of God. The ear, the hand, the legs, the tongue, and all other limbs are trusts that must be maintained."

5. Finally, the trust has been interpreted as "divine commands, such as prayers, fasting, and the obligatory pilgrimage."[7]

And there are many more interpretations. If we reflect on all these interpretations, we see that they can all be combined under one heading. We can say that the trust consists of "responsibility and obligations; in other words, the trust is what vests responsibility in a creation to carry on its obligations and observe the law."[8]

MAN AND THE TRUST

This great and heavy trust was offered to all creations before it was finally given to mankind. Some may imagine that each creation had a choice of taking the trust or refusing it. They assume that all creation had equal abilities and each was given a choice. However, the reality of the matter is that every creation has a different set of abilities and capabilities. The verse is describing the state of these beings and what they are effectively "saying" (by virtue of their existence) given the nature of their abilities. Hence, when the trust was offered to creations that do not have the proper abilities to carry the trust, they declared their inability to bear it. Each creation besides man had a "weakness of heart" when it was offered the trust because of its inability to bear it.

---

[7] Al-Shirazi, *Al-Amthal*, 13:368.

[8] Al-Mutahhari, *Al-Islam wa Mutatalibat al-Asr*, 21.

But there was also the role of man. This majestic creation that, despite his weakness, has a great deal of abilities that allows him to stand out amongst creations. Mankind declared that it would bear this trust that God offered. They would be God's agents. They would be the focal-point of creation. They would exhibit servitude and worship out of their free will. They would carry the profound responsibility. Therein lies the greatness of mankind. God says, *"Certainly We have honored the Children of Adam, and carried them over land and sea, and provided them with all the good things, and preferred them with a complete preference over many of those We have created."*[9] This is why mankind was worthy of the angels' prostration.

> *When your Lord said to the angels, 'Indeed I am going to create a human out of a dry clay [drawn] from an aging mud. So when I have proportioned him and breathed into him of My spirit, then fall down in prostration before him.' Thereat the angels prostrated, all of them together.*[10]

In this verse, we see another form of honor that is bestowed on mankind. God created man's soul and honored it to such an extent that He attributed it to Himself, in the Arabic language, saying "My spirit" (the spirit which God created).This, no doubt, is part of the reason for which mankind took on this great responsibility. All of this shows us the greatness of mankind and its position compared to all other creation. It is the only creation that can ascend on the infinite stairway of perfection. All other creations behave in accordance with their innate nature; what is sometimes called "creational guidance" that God imbued in every being

---

[9] The Holy Quran. Chapter 17 [The Ascension; Arabic: *Al-Mi'raj*]. Verse 70.
[10] The Holy Quran. Chapter 15 [Arabic: *Al-Hijr*]. Verses 28-30.

at the moment of creation. Each being exists in accordance
to that nature that God has given it without attempting to
improve its life or change the order in which it exists. Let's
take honeybees as an example. The type of life that they live
does not witness the same type of advancement and excellence possible in human existence. For thousands of years,
they have been living in the same way. Their intricate social
order did not change. God says,

> *And your Lord inspired the bee [saying]: 'Make your home
> in the mountains, and on the trees and the trellises that they
> erect. Then eat from every [kind of] fruit and follow meekly
> the ways of your Lord.' There issues from its belly a juice of
> diverse hues, in which there is a cure for the people. There is
> indeed a sign in that for a people who reflect.*[11]

The same situation applies to the sun and the moon, which
have not changed in their general motion.

> *The sun runs on to its place of rest: That is the ordaining of
> the All-mighty, the All-knowing. As for the moon, We
> have ordained its phases, until it becomes like an old palm
> leaf. Neither it behooves the sun to overtake the moon, nor
> may the night outrun the day, and each swims in an orbit.*[12]

Therefore, each creation has its distinct nature and none of
them can ascend the levels of moral excellence like mankind. Mankind, as opposed to all other creation, lives in a
state of constant change and progress. We have the ability
to seek and attain different forms of perfection. We are not
bound to our natural instinct, but rather we can look be-

---

[11] The Holy Quran. Chapter 16 [The Bees; Arabic: *Al-Nahl*]. Verses 68, 69.
[12] The Holy Quran. Chapter 36 [Arabic: *Yaseen*]. Verses 38-40.

yond it. God has not given us concrete paths that we cannot develop past. Rather, his commands have come in the form of legislation. We have the power to obey or disobey these commands. *"Indeed We have guided him to the way, be he grateful or ungrateful."*[13]

So we see that man is able to ascend in levels of perfection and use his God-given abilities to be in a position where he is worthy of the prostration of the angels. If he is ungrateful and disobedient, he descends to the rank of other animals or even lower. God says of the ungrateful, *"they are just like cattle; indeed, they are further astray from the way."*[14]

BEARING THE TRUST

When mankind took on this trust, was he able to bear it properly? Did he fulfill this great responsibility?

Here, we must discuss two important points that will answer these questions. In other words, we must look at mankind from two different perspectives to be able to answer these questions.

Man the Genus

When we look at mankind as a genus, we see that it was able to bear and fulfill this responsibility. Collectively, we have been able to reach the highest levels of perfection. We have been able to reach certainty and knowledge of God. This was achieved through the prophets, their immaculate successors, and the righteous believers. They lead mankind's journey towards perfection and they reached the ultimate

---

[13] The Holy Quran. Chapter 76 [Man; Arabic: *Al-Insan*]. Verse 3.
[14] The Holy Quran. Chapter 25 [Arabic: *Al-Furqan*]. Verse 44.

goal. This is evident in the verse above. The angels, one of God's greatest creations, prostrated to the perfect man who had learned "the Names" and taught them to the angels. So collectively, we have been able to reach the highest levels of perfection.

Man the Individual

When we look at mankind as individuals, we will find that the overwhelming majority of us have not lived up to this great responsibility that we were given. We abandoned the trust. We were given the faculties of intellect, will, and choice, but we did not use them to seek perfection. On the contrary, we have used these faculties for our own deviation and degeneracy.

Here, the verse comes to show us this reality that we have reached as individuals, due to our own mistakes, irrationality, and weakness. That is why the verse referred to him as "*most unjust and ignorant.*"[15] In the Arabic language, the mode in which the phrase was used indicates aggrandizement of the characteristics – God is emphasizing the great deal of injustice and ignorance that we have brought down upon ourselves by accepting the responsibility of the trust but not living up to the task. that reflects the reality that we live in when we abandon the highest states of perfection that we can achieve to live a lowly and wretched life through attachment to the pleasures of this world. We commit a great injustice when we deny ourselves life in the divine realms, with all its pleasures and closeness to God, only to live the life of cattle that care only for their materialistic desires.

---

15 The Holy Quran. Chapter 33 [The Factions; Arabic: *Al-Ahzab*]. Verse 72.

What ignorance is greater than selling the hereafter for the sake of this world? Selling eternal bliss for temporal and fleeting pleasures?

Therefore we see that most people did not fulfill this responsibility. We did not make full use of the status and faculties that God has given us. Instead of attempting to reach the state where the angels would prostrate to us, we ourselves have prostrated to our own whims and desires. We have taken things that we have made with our own hands as idols. Therefore, mankind is most unjust and ignorant, not because we have accepted the great responsibility and trust that God has given us, but because we have not lived up them.

CONSEQUENCES OF THE TRUST

After addressing how mankind accepted the responsibility for the trust, the Quran goes on to mention the following: *"God will surely punish the hypocrites, men and women, and the polytheists, men and women, and God will turn clemently to the faithful, men and women, and God is all-forgiving, all-merciful."*[16]

Here interpreters of the Quran have deduced two possibilities for the relationship between the two verses. Some interpreters said that the second verse is addressing the consequences of mankind's acceptance of the trust. They say that mankind's acceptance of the trust resulted in three consequences upon which individuals can be categorized. Some individuals acted hypocritically towards the trust or disbelieved in God altogether. These two groups will be pun-

---

[16] Ibid, Verses 72, 73.

ished. As for the third group who fulfilled the responsibility of the trust, they will be blessed with God's mercy and rewards.

Another group of interpreters have suggested that the second verse is addressing the reasons for which the trust was given to mankind in the first place. They say God wants to tell us that he gave us this trust so he can test us, and so that each person gets the opportunity to act accordingly and deserve punishment and reward for his actions.

Either way, the end result is the same. People can be categorized into groups based on how they deal with the trust. Some are able to use the trust as a means to ascend in levels of perfection; while others neglect the trust and only descend in ranks of degeneracy.

The Degenerate

The Quran describes the degenerates who did not fulfill the responsibility of the trust and did not use God's blessings to fulfill that responsibility as hypocrites and disbelievers. They are divided into two groups because some of those degenerates showed outwardly their abandonment of the responsibility that came with the trust, and those are the disbelievers. The other group were called hypocrites because they concealed their degenerate nature and tried to show themselves as authentic keepers of the divine trust. Their degeneracy is even greater because of their dishonesty, and so their punishment will be more severe.

The Ascendant

The ascendants are those who have fulfilled the responsibility of the trust and obeyed the commands of God. Although they differ in the degree in which they met their responsibility, they will all gain the mercy of God. God will turn clemently to them and grant them mercy. They are most fearful of sin, and so God comforts them with his assurance that they will attain His mercy. They made use of their position, fulfilled their responsibility, and maintained God's trust. The indubitable result will be forgiveness, reward, and paradise.

Man and Woman

You might have noticed that whenever the verse mentioned any of the degenerate categories or the ascendants, it referred to them as both men and women. The reason for this is to draw our attention to the fact that men and women are at an equal footing when it comes to this trust. Both genders carry the trust and both will be held accountable. Ascendance through the levels of perfection is possible for both men and women. The Quran and the narrations hold in high regards those women that ascended through the levels of perfection, such as the Lady Mary (a) mother of Prophet Jesus, Asiya (a) the wife of Pharaoh, Lady Khadija (a) the wife of Prophet Muhammad (s), and – of course – the Lady of Light, Lady Fatima (a).

SYNOPSIS

In summary, we believe that mankind is among the greatest of all creations. He holds, despite his feeble physique, abilities and potential that allowed him to carry the divine trust. He was given the opportunity to make use of these God-given abilities to fulfill the responsibility of this trust. If he were to do so, he would win the greatest of rewards. He would earn the eternal rewards that come with pleasing God and being in true servitude to Him. He will live in the bliss of knowing God and feel the happiness of being close to Him.

Not using the abilities that God has given us to fulfill this responsibility will be the greatest injustice that we can inflict upon ourselves. The greatest ignorance lies in being heedless of this great opportunity.

Oh God! Make us of those who were given your trust and knew how to carry it, and praise be to You, Oh Lord of the Worlds.

A RELATIONSHIP WITH GOD

In the Name of God, the most Beneficent, the most Merciful

Say, 'If you love God, then follow me; God will love you and forgive you your sins, and God is all-forgiving, all-merciful.' [1]

Man in his creation is weak and dependent, not owning any independent power or strength. There is not a single instance in the life of man, where he is completely independent and not reliant on the kindness and generosity of God. We, as human beings, are unable to produce even the simplest things without the help and mercy of God that has encompassed everything. This is one aspect to consider.

Another aspect to consider is that God wants mankind to fulfill his obligation of servitude, because he created mankind with the purpose of worship. From this premise the individual stands before a split in roads or a number of different types of worship. Worship here means obedience and

---

[1] The Holy Quran. Chapter 3 [Arabic: *Aal Imran*]. Verse 31.

adherence to everything that God wants and abstaining from all that he has forbidden.

Therefore, is simply adherening and not transgressing against the rules of God considered sufficient? And by that adherence and lack of transgression would one be considered to have fulfilled his servitude to God? Or is true servitude to God characteristic of a specific quality that transcends this and truly satisfies the Creator and His divinely ordained purpose for mankind?

There are a number of discussion points in this particular topic:

OUR RELATIONSHIP WITH GOD

We find ourselves before a number of various types of worship as narrated to us by the Ahlulbayt (a). Some people worship God in fear of His punishment, because God has promised those who disobey Him with stark chastisement. Others worship God desiring His reward, because God also promised those who adhere to His guidance with paradise. However, there is a third group of people who worship God simply because they love Him. They do not worship God because they are scared of punishment nor due to their desire of his grand reward of paradise. The driving force of worship here is love.

Imam Al-Sadiq (a) said:

> *Servants of God are of three kinds: 1) people who worship God out fear – that is the worship of slaves; 2) people who worship God seeking reward – that is the worship of mer-*

chants; and 3) people who worship God out of love for Him
— that is the worship of free men, and the best of worship.[2]

There is no doubt that the third type of worship is the finest type of worship due to the following reasons:

In a number of the verses in the Holy Quran, God instructs us to worship Him with sincerity and have faith in him: *"Though they were not commanded except to worship God, dedicating their faith to Him as men of pure faith…"*[3] We can't truly imagine what sincerity in worship truly is unless we detach our hearts from everything, both matters of this life and the afterlife. The only thing that such a person links or attaches to in worship is God and nothing else. That heart must be filled with the true love for God, because sincerity cannot be built without true love.

Allama Al-Tabatabaei (q) says, "Love is the only means to tie every supplicant with who he supplicates to and every needy with who he needs."[4] As human beings we feel lacking or deficient in so many things. There is no way to take care of that feeling except means that fulfill that lacking and plug that deficiency. Thus, we are pulled towards the things that help us take care of our deficiencies. This rule applies in a number of different examples. We prepare food and eat to satisfy our hunger. We seek out friends to fulfill our desire for company and companionship. In our relationship with God, if we are able to worship Him in a state of sincerity we wouldn't have a worry in this world except that God love us and be pleased with us. Through being loved, we satisfy our

[2] Al-Kulayni, *Al-Kafi*, 2:84.
[3] The Holy Quran. Chapter 98 [Arabic: *Al-Bayyina*]. Verse 5.
[4] Al-Tabatabaei, *Al-Mizan*, 3:158.

need of obedience and submissiveness to the will of God. A true servant of God is one who does not find any satisfaction or comfort except by completely pleasing God. This only happens through the true love between the servant and his Lord. If anything else were to leech on in this relationship, then the true worship of sincerity will not come to fruition, nor would pure faith in Him be realized. Imam Al-Sadiq (a) said, *"A man does not have pure faith in God until God becomes more dear and beloved to the man than himself, his father, his mother, his children, his family, his wealth, and everyone else."*[5]

Ahlulbayt (a) greatly focused on this topic of love for God in their supplications, because to them this love means everything. Imam Zain Al-Abideen (a) calls onto his Lord through his following words:

> *O' my Lord… Even if You tied me with chains, and You deprived me from Your flowing stream (of favors) amongst the witnesses (of the Day of Judgment); and divulge all my scandalous acts before the eyes of all Your servants; and You order me to hell, and You isolate me from the company of the faithful; I would not lose my hope in You, and I would not dismiss my reassurance of Your pardon, and my love for You would never leave my heart…*[6]

In another part of the same supplication, the Imam (a) says: *"O' my Lord… I ask You to fill my heart with Your love, fearing and observing You, believing in Your (holy) book, having faith in*

---

[5] Al-Majlisi, *Bihar Al-Anwar*, 67:25.

[6] Al-Tusi, *Misbaah Al-Mujtahid*, 590.

You, fearing You, and longing for You... O' [You who is] the One full of majesty, bounty and honor?"[7]

GOD'S LOVE

Having the love of God and filling your heart with such pure love may be easier said than done. This may require spiritual discipline, hard work, and dedication to ensure that nothing lies in that heart but the pure love of God. If this heart were to love anyone or anything it would only be through and for the love of God. God orders us to love the works of God and His emissaries, and to love those who are dear to God and His servants. Our love for them in turn springs from our love for Him – our true love. Some of the ways that helps us reach this love include the following:

First, contemplating over the bounties and blessings of God. People are often too heedless of God's blessings upon them, to the point where they forget their essence and purpose of their existence. We can very easily take what we have for granted because of how easily accessible it is and forget God's favors upon us. When we do take a moment to think about these blessings, and their importance to us, our hearts are bound to gravitate to the One who honored us with all these blessings. That is why we find so many of the supplications by Ahlulbayt (a) emphasizing the importance of not forgetting the bounties and blessings of God. Take this excerpt from Dua Al-Jawshan Al-Sagheer, by Imam Moussa Al-Kadhim (a), for example:

---

[7] Ibid.

...Bless Muhammad and the Household of Muhammad, and include me with those who are thankful for Your bounties, and those who permanently mention Your graces. Have mercy upon me, by Your mercy, O most Merciful of all those who show mercy...[8]

Remembrance of God's blessings and bounties are repeated throughout chapter 55 of the Holy Quran, *"So which of your Lord's bounties will you both deny?"*[9]

Contemplation is instrumental in deepening our love for God. Ahlulbayt (a) emphasized this time and time again. We see a clear example of this through the words of the Holy Prophet (s): *"Love God for all the blessings he nurtures you with. Love me for the love of God, and love my Household for my love."*[10]

Secondly, refining the self to worship out of the drive of love, which can be achieved by having your complete focus on God. Avoid performing acts of worship – like prayer, fasting, and supplication – with the purpose of simply receiving good deeds and reward. Instead, approacjh your worship because God wants it for us. It is significant to pay close attention to this because it has big effect on the level and status of that person with God. By emphasizing this practice, to worship God regardless of the reward and with only God's love in mind, a person gets to a point where he doesn't want anything in this world but God. *"We feed you only for the sake of God. We desire no reward from you, nor*

---

[8] Al-Majlisi, *Bihar Al-Anwar*, 91:317.

[9] The Holy Quran. Chapter 55 [Arabic: *Al-Rahman*]. Verse 13.

[10] Al-Sadouq, *'Ilel Al-Shara'i*, 1:139.

thanks."[11] The more focus you place on this perspective and intention, the deeper you will fall in love with God.

Thirdly, to empty the heart from any connection or link to anything other than God. Love for God cannot be combined with love for anything else. Imam Al-Sadiq (a) says: *"The heart is the sanctuary of God, so do not allow anyone but God in that sanctuary."*[12] So long as the heart is busy with the matters of this worldly life, it will not be cleared for true devotion to God. If that is so, then what is the position of the heart that is busy with not only worldly matters but with things that God detests? A person cannot bring the love of God and what God dislikes in the same heart. You cannot claim to love God and love the things that he detests. If you love God, then to the extent that you love Him you would love what He loves and loathe what He loathes. Thus, we see Imam Al-Sadiq (a) saying, *"I asked for the love of God, and I found it in opposing the people of sin."*[13]

A person will not find the sweetness of God's love in his heart until he empties heart completely from the matters of this world that conflict with the love of God. Imam Al-Sadiq (a) also said in this regard, *"If a person renounces this world, he will find the sweet love of God..."*[14]

Fourthly, there is always an underlying reason for our love, or lack thereof, of someone or something. That reason goes back to a person's nature or temperament. Some aspects of

---

[11] The Holy Quran. Chapter 76 [Arabic: *Al-Naziat*]. Verse 9.

[12] Al-Majlisi, *Bihar Al-Anwar*, 67:25.

[13] Al-Reishahri, *Mizan Al-Hikma*, 1:503. Citing, Al-Nouri, *Mustadrak Al-Wasail*, 12:173.

[14] Al-Kulayni, *Al-Kafi*, 2:130.

that may be due to our inherent dispositions and other aspects are due to the accumulated impact of our exercise of free will, as we make good or bad choices. Our temperament can often be a significant determinant of what we are drawn to or what turns us away. Our innate nature pushes us to sync with that which meshes well with our temperament. For example, our innate nature draws us to love certain foods because the taste of that food is appealing to our disposition. Likewise, we like certain flowers because their fragrance is also pleasing to our nature. If we were able to derive the taste and fragrance without the actual food or flower, we would have no inclination or attraction to those items. Thus, here is the truth in the matter: there does not exist in this world anything that is more appealing, attractive, befitting, and harmonious with the innate nature and disposition of the human being other than God. He is the closest thing to us, "… *and We are nearer to him than his jugular vein.*"[15]

Anything that is harmonious with one's nature and inclines him to have love for it, is an overabundance of blessings from God. Thus, when a person attaches his heart to God he becomes sufficient from needing to love anything else. But at the same time, his heart becomes full of love for all of God's creation. The love of God is like light, the closer you are to his love the greater the warmth and illumination you will feel.[16]

---

[15] The Holy Quran. Chapter 50 [Arabic: *Qaf*]. Verse 16.
[16] Rufai'i, *Tazkiyat An-Nafs wa Tahtheeb Al-Rooh*, 143.

THE MANIFESTATIONS OF THE LOVE OF GOD

It is not enough for us to simply say that we love God; instead we need to show it. To proclaim love for God is not the essence of love, Ahlulbayt (a) show us what the manifestations of that love are:

Communicating with God

One of the signs for having love for God is having a passion for communicating with God through worshipping, remembering, and striving towards Him. Think about it. How can a person claim love for another when he gets annoyed in the other's presence or becomes bored when talking to them? A person who is in love longs for the company of his beloved. When you see your beloved your eyes light up, your heart palpitates, your whole existence is moved and boredom could not possibly be fathomed in their presence.

> *God spoke to Moses son of Imran (a) and said: 'O' son of Imran, the one who claims to love me but when night falls sleeps without remembering me has lied. Does not every lover long for the company of his beloved? I am here, O' son of Imran, looking over my loved ones. If the night falls upon them, their hearts are not distracted [from Me] by what their eyes see, my punishment would manifest before their sight, they address me out of vision, and they speak to me out of presence. O' son of Imran give me the piety of your heart, the obedience of your body, and the tears of your eyes in the darkness of the night. Call on to me, you will find me near answering your call.*[17]

---

[17] Al-Sadouq, *Al-Amaali*, 438.

Obeying God

The sign of true love is being completely content with your loved one and being compliant to what he wants of you. True love means you accept and are content with your beloved. But for a person to claim that he loves, while he doesn't accept the words of his beloved, nor does he do what he asks, then that is not true love.

> *One who disobeys and sins against God does not truly love Him… Do you disobey God as you proclaim your love for Him? This is surely an innovative way of showing love… If your love for Him was true, you would have obeyed Him. True love is claimed by those who obey their beloved.*[18]

Moreover, true love is that which the lover feels a shortcoming in doing well by the right of his beloved. He feels that he is not doing enough for his beloved, in comparison to how much he truly loves Him.

Reflecting Love Onto Others

Of the manifestations of the love of God, one of its signs is the reflection of God's love in loving everything that God Himself loves. So, the lover of God will only love things that God loves and despise only the things that God despises and detests. He will not love anything that God detests, nor will he detest anything that God loves.

True love for God shows in that a person will love *by* God and detest *by* God. The Holy Prophet (s) said to some of his companions: *"O' servant of God, love by God and detest by God. Befriend by God and rival by God. You will not receive the guardian-*

---

[18] Ibid, 578.

ship of God except by that, nor will any man taste faith with all his prayers and fasts except by this way...[19]

Imam Al-Baqir (a) also provides this measure in the following tradition:

> *If you want to know if there is any good in you, look at your heart. If your heart loves the people of obedience to God and despises the people of sin, then within you is goodness and God loves you. However, if your heart detests the people of obedience to God and loves the people of sin, then there is no goodness in you and God detests you. For man is with who he loves.*[20]

Following the Role Models

If a person wants to show his love for God, there is no doubt that he should display it by way of the vicegerents that God has obliged humanity to follow. *"Say, 'If you love God, then follow me; God will love you and forgive you your sins, and God is all-forgiving, all-merciful.'"*[21] It is not enough for a person to claim that he loves God without loving and following the Prophet (s) as well. Furthermore , it is not enough to just love the Prophet (s) and his successors, but one must follow them and take them as role models so that God is pleased. Thus, we notice the constant connection between obedience to God and obedience to his emissaries and representatives, and the love of God and the love of his emissaries and representatives. Take the following excerpt from Ziyarat Al-Jami'a: "*He who obeys you in fact obeys God, and he who disobeys*

---

[19] Al-Sadouq, *Ma'ani Al-Akhbar*, 399.

[20] Rufai'i, *Tazkiyat An-Nafs wa Tahtheeb Al-Rooh*, 144. Citing, Al-Kashani, *Al-Waafee*, 90.

[21] The Holy Quran. Chapter 3 [Arabic: *Aal Imran*]. Verse 31.

you in fact disobeys God. He who loves you in fact loves God, and he who hates you in fact hates God. He who holds onto you has in fact held on to God..."[22]

The scale and correct measure of the love for God is the love for the Holy Prophet (s) and his Ahlulbayt (a), and how dedicated one is in following their example. It is from here that we understand the wondrous expressions and robust rewards for those who love the Household of Muhammad (s). In the following tradition, the Holy Prophet (s) says:

He who dies in the love of Ahlulbayt dies the death of a martyr. He who dies in the love of Ahlulbayt is forgiven his sins. He who dies in the love of Ahlulbayt dies in repentance. He who dies in the love of Ahlulbayt dies a believer with complete faith. He who dies in the love of Ahlulbayt, is given the glad tidings of paradise by the Angel of Death and the Angels Munkar and Nakeer. He who dies in the love of Ahlulbayt is walked into paradise in celebration like the celebration of a bride that is walked into her new home. He who dies in the love of Ahlulbayt will have two doors to paradise opened for him in his grave. He who dies in the love of Ahlulbayt, God will make his grave a shrine for the Angels of mercy. He who dies in the love of Ahlulbayt has died on the path of the prophetic tradition. And he who dies with hatred towards Ahlulbayt, will come on the Day of Judgment with hopelessness written between his eyes. He who dies with hatred towards Ahlulbayt dies as a disbeliever. He who dies with hatred towards Ahlulbayt will never smell the fragrance of paradise.[23]

---

[22] Al-Tusi, *Al-Tahtheeb*, 6:101.

[23] Al-Majlisi, *Bihar Al-Anwar*, 23:233; Al-Zamkhashri, *Tafseer Al-Kashaf*, 3:467.

There are numerous narrations similar to the one above. There is no doubt that this Household would not have such a status without their closeness to God. He sent them to us to guide and save us from ruin. God made them as a scale and measure for our love for Him. In essence, one who knows Muhammad (s) and his Household (a), yet does not have love for them in his heart, does not have an atom's worth of love for God the Almighty.

DIVINE JUSTICE

In the Name of God, the most Beneficent, the most Merciful

No affliction visits the land or yourselves but it is in a Book before We bring it about – that is indeed easy for God – so that you may not grieve for what escapes you, nor boast for what comes your way, and God does not like any swaggering braggart.[1]

With our tests and trials throughout life on Earth, our communities and cultures have collectively asked questions regarding the system of creation. These questions have boggled the minds of so many across decades and centuries. To this day, these issues remain alive in heated discussions of philosophy and science. So many societies and cultures have asked the following: Why did God create tragedies and evil in this world? Wouldn't the world have been so much more beautiful without all of these tragedies and tribulations? Couldn't God prevent all the hurt and evil from happening? Couldn't He have made Earth filled with only blessings and goodness, instead of having evil, pain and suffering? These

---

[1] The Holy Quran. Chapter 57 [The Iron; Arabic: *Al-Hadeed*]. Verses 22-23.

are questions people have posed across generations in an attempt to deal with this issue:

We will discuss a few points in order for us to answer these complex questions. Through these points we can give a summary of the philosophy of evil and the tragedies that afflict people in their lives. One chapter is simply not enough to delve into all the details of this study and would need much more explanation and emphasis than a few pages. Nonetheless, we will try to shed some light on this intricate issue in a way that can benefit the reader who has pondered these questions.

PHILOSOPHIES ON EVIL

Just as the problem of evil has made its way as a major issue in the discourse of societies across history, the solution to this problem has been a similarly important issue. Philosophers, jurists, and religious scholars have all tried to propose solutions to this issue. Amongst all the propositions, the three most important theories involved in resolving this issue are the following:

Denying the Wise Creator

There are a group of people who have found themselves unable to fully understand the complexity of this issue, pondering: how could there be harmony between the ideas that there exists a wise creator and a system that is plagued with evils, tragedies and tribulations? Thus, to deal with this seemingly incoherent combination, this group did away with the idea that there exists a wise creator; rather, matter itself was the first being or always has existed. This approach represents incompetence in thought and a mere excuse that provides no solution to the initial issue at hand. If denying or negating the existence of God is proposed as a solution to the problem of evil, then it creates an even greater issue for us. We enter a discourse that questions the entirety of existence, its origin, and creation. The ultimate source of existence cannot conceivably have any deficiencies, let alone a lack in something as significant as wisdom. Thus, this proposed idea does not actually solve anything; instead it only provides a scapegoat.

The Existence of Two Creators

Some cultures and religions have accepted this theory, due to their inability to deal with their proposition that God could be the source for both good and evil. Thus, they proposed that there exists two gods – the god of light that emits goodness and the god of darkness that emits evil. The god of light causes all the good in the world, and all the evil in the world is caused by the god of darkness. This theory is unacceptable because of the necessity of oneness in the nature of the Origin of the universe. If two gods were to exist, they would compete and affect each other's power, authority and influence upon the rest of creation. This conflicts directly with the necessity for the Ultimate Cause – God – to be one who is incomparable to anything else and beyond everything else, which he created and is the cause of. The evidence and proof for the existence of a single origin, one creator, the cause of all causes, is overwhelming; this is especially when compared to the proposition that there exists two competing gods.

The Inexistence and Relativity of Evil

The proposition of the inexistence and relativity of evil is one that mostly people of monotheistic faith affiliate with. Furthermore, this theory has roots in the deep history of Greek philosophy with particular focus by Plato. Nonetheless, theologians have analyzed and detailed this theory with much more depth. This analysis has relied on two primary bases:

The Absolute Inexistence of Evil

In using the word 'inexistence' we can refer to it in two different meanings. The first meaning for inexistence is in the absolute sense. This is in opposition to absolute existence; thus, anything that contradicts existence is called inexistence. The second meaning for inexistence of evil is not in the absolute sense; rather it is the attribute used to describe things that have lost something of their essence. Think of something that becomes corrupted or spoiled, deficiencies, shameful acts, diseases and pain. All of these things are examples of this meaning of inexistence, being one that is a description of the lacking of a person's or a thing's complete nature.[2] In essence, evil is the lack or absence of good. Hence, evil could not have been understood as an attribute without the existence of good.

Thus, when we discuss the inexistence of evil we are referring to the second meaning because we do believe that evil actually does exist in a sense. We can't say that evil does not exist in the absolute sense; rather, it exists in the sense that it is the lack or absence of good. Take the following exam-

---

[2] Al-Haydari, *Al-Tawheed*, 2:283. Citing, Al-Tabatabaei, *Al-Mizan*, 13:188.

ples: blindness is the lack of sight; darkness is the lack of light; and the cold is the lack of energy or heat. The former attributes do not exist in the absolute sense; instead they are present as the lack or absence of something else. Philosophers have provided intellectual proofs in support of the second meaning we have referred to. In this discussion we will bring forth some of these proofs in a simplified manner as to not convolute an already complex subject. If we were to look at all of the things we call evil, they negate the existence of another thing. Look at the examples of plague, disease, killing, and natural disasters like earthquakes and hurricanes, which are all causes of death and the end of physical life. From another aspect, the things we describe as evil can be things that negate the completeness of another existent thing (as opposed to negating the entire existence of the being). Consider the following examples: ignorance as the negation of knowledge, poverty as the negation of wealth, and illness as the negation of health. Thus, evil can be the absence of something's very existence or the incompleteness of something that exists.

Allama Al-Hilli says,

> *If we were to contemplate over the things which are attributed as evil, we would find that they are simply the absence of something that exists. Don't you see murder? People have determined that it is evil, and if we are to think about it we would find its evilness in what absence it has brought. There is no evil in a person's ability to act, for ability and power is part of the excellence of mankind. Nor is it that the sharpness of the instrument espouses evil because sharpness is an attribute that brings forth the brilliance of the instrument.*

Evil is also not in the movement of the individuals' limbs towards the act, nor is it in the tenderness of one's flesh that so easily receives the blade. Rather, evil is in cutting short the innately good attribute, which is life. Evil is nothing but the absence of good... Thus, people have judged that existence is absolute good and inexistence is absolute evil.[3]

What we see as evil is not evil in its essence, but it is described as evil because it is the absence of something that exists or that existent thing's completeness. If we come to this conclusion, then it would be incorrect to ask: why did God create evil? Evil is an attribute of absence, and thus is not created. Furthermore, the other premise of the existence of good versus the existence of evil is also incorrect. Our world does not have two opposing existences, which would then seemingly require two origins and two creators, as imposed by one of the aforementioned theories of existence. In reality, there is only one form of existence: good. Everything that is considered evil is only, in essence, the absence of good. Evil is the absence of good, just as darkness is the absence of light. When we observe that the primary source of light in our world is the sun, can we also observe a source of darkness? The sun emits light, but what emits darkness? Darkness is not emitted nor is it produced by any independent source because, in reality, it only exists as the absence of light.[4]

On this similar basis, we cannot differentiate evil as a category fully distinct and independent from good. Though we can differentiate between inanimate objects and plants, and

[3] Al-Hilli, *Kashf Al-Murad fe Sharh Tajreed Al-I'tiqad*, 12.
[4] Al-Mutahhari, *Al-'Adl Al-Ilahi*, 161.

between plants and animals as distinct categories, we cannot differentiate between good and evil in the same way. There is no class of existing beings that can be identified by their very meaning to be pure evil with absolutely no good. Evil is linked to Good; you can't disconnect evil from some level of good. Wherever you see evil in nature, you will also see good. Existence and its absence, in reality, do not form two disconnected and distinct categories. Absence is only the lack of the existent, and so long as there is existence, utter absence cannot prevail.

The Relativity of Evil

From the examples that we discussed earlier we can conclude two types of evil. One, what is essentially the absence of something that exists like ignorance, disability, and poverty. These states of being are real, but describe the absence of knowledge, ability, and wealth – elements that are existent. Two, things that in reality do exist as independent entities but are described as evil, like a snake or a scorpion. The scorpion is an existent living thing, but because it is a cause of harm to a human being it is described as evil. Similarly, earthquakes could be considered evil because they naturally cause destruction to habitats, human beings and animals.

In examining the second meaning, things are described as evil when they are measured in relation to creatures or things. For example, the poison of a scorpion is not evil to the scorpion itself – it is actually pure good for the scorpion. Though its poison is evil to a human being, it is not evil to inanimate objects and plants because they are not affected by the scorpion's poison. Similarly, a wolf would be considered as evil to a sheep but not evil to a plant (unless the wolf eats the plant). The plant would consider the sheep evil, but as human beings we see no evil in sheep. The perspective of what is evil and what isn't is based on how that particular party is being affected by the thing in question, not that the thing is evil in its essence.

> *There is nothing that exists that is considered evil by its own self; rather, things are only considered evil in relation to others. There is no doubt, as well, that true and real existence is that which exists itself. With regards to circumstantial existence, it is relative and conceptual and thus does not exist in reality beyond concept. So it doesn't really exist for you to even ask the question: why were these particular things given relative existence?[5]*

And on these two bases, the concept of duality in origin and existence for good and evil is refuted. In essence, there only exists pure good and evil is simply the absence of that good or a measure of relativity that has no actual existence.

Nonetheless, the problem remains: human beings still suffer from the issue of evil, regardless if it were an attribute of absence or relativity. Mankind still suffers from ignorance, poverty, blindness and death. Why is one person blind, another is deaf, while a third is born with deformities? The answer to these questions can be found in the discussions under the next two headings.

THE CURRENT ORDER

Muslims believe that the current order of the universe and existence is the best possible system. We cannot imagine a

---

[5] Ibid, 166.

better system of order than the one that we have. This inference is made by both logical and scriptural proof.

Logical Proof

The logical proof in this discussion is built on three premises that will drive us to our conclusion:

1. God is the all-knowing. His knowledge is infinite and encompasses all things with no limit.

2. God is capable of manifesting what He knows, and creates or converts what is known in his knowledge to an outside reality. He is capable of anything, which is essential and proven as a characteristic of His oneness. If the concept is within the scope of possibility God is capable of it. In regards to that which is impossible in its essence then that has nothing to do with God's ability, because it is not possible in its essence to even be considered within the domain of ability.

3. Given that God has the knowledge and the ability, there is nothing that could prevent God from manifesting what is in His knowledge into the outside reality. If there is nothing imaginable that could possibly stand in His way and these premises of knowledge and ability are sound, then it would naturally follow that God would only manifest into reality what is the most excellent and complete – the best order. To postulate that God would manifest something that is deficient or even merely adequate, instead of what is best, is proposing a notion with no weight. Such a proposition is logically impossible for the perfect nature of God. There is no reason

for God to choose the good option as opposed to the best option. It is only reasonable to deduce, therefore, that God created the universe in the best possible order.

Textual Proof

The Holy Quran and the noble traditions clearly illustrate that our system of order is exceptionally unmatched: "*You see the mountains, which you suppose, to be stationary, while they drift like passing clouds—the handiwork of God who has made everything faultless. He is indeed well aware of what you do.*"[6]

> *It is God who created the heavens and the earth and whatever is between them in six days, then He settled on the Throne. You do not have besides Him any guardian or intercessor. Will you not then take admonition? He directs the command from the heaven to the earth; then it ascends toward Him in a day whose span is a thousand years by your reckoning. That is the Knower of the sensible and the Unseen, the All-mighty, the All-merciful, who perfected everything that He created and commenced man's creation from clay.*[7]

The Commander of the Faithful (a) said,

> *He has created and fixed limits for everything, and made those limits firm. He has secured its working and made the working delicate. He has fixed its direction and it does not transgress the bounds of its position nor fall short of reaching the end of its aim… Thus, He straightened the curves of the things and fixed their confines. With His power He cre-*

---

[6] The Holy Quran. Chapter 27 [The Ants; Arabic: *Al-Naml*]. Verse 88.
[7] The Holy Quran. Chapter 32 [Arabic: *Al-Sajda*]. Verses 4-7.

ated coherence in their contradictory parts and amalgamated
the factors of similarity. Then, He separated them in varie-
ties, which differ in limits, quantities, properties and shapes.
All of this is new creation. He invented them, firm and
shaped as He wished.[8]

There are numerous narrations similar to this one that point
to the mastery and perfection of God's creation and provisions. Thus, the logical and textual proofs have established
that this order is the best and most complete and there
could not possibly be one greater.

Nonetheless, the question then ensues: if this is the best and
most complete order, then why does it have pain, suffering,
and evil? If we consider this evil as simply a description of
absence or a matter of relativity that is only circumstantial
and conceptual as mentioned, was God not capable of de-
signing the world of possibility in a way that excluded the
relativity of evil? In other words: what exists in this world is
purely good, yet there are absences, inexistences, or lacking
to which we described as relative conceptual existences. So
why didn't God create a world where there was no absence
or lacking? Why didn't he substitute the lack of existence
with more existence? The answer to this is in the next point.

SOLVING THE DILEMMA

Here we'll address and resolve a problem that differs from
the first. In the first issue we discussed the problem of the
creation of evil. The answer to that was: evil is not created;

---

[8] Al-Radi, *Nahjul Balagha*, 1:165, Sermon 91 (Known as the Sermon of Phan-
toms).

evil is simply the absence of existence. This differs from the second issue where we concluded that: the system and order God has created for us is the best possible order to exist. However, both the first and second resolutions don't address the third issue, which is the following: what is the purpose or reason behind the relative existence of evil?

Why didn't God create us with everlasting lives instead of mortals that experienced death? Why didn't he create us with lasting health instead of having the experience of disease and illness? Scholars have answered this questioning in three ways:

The Material World

The material world cannot be without contradiction and conflict, because it involves beings who have the ability to seek progress and perfection. This can't happen without conflict between existent beings. Trees cannot grow without affecting the ground around them; animals cannot develop without eating the fruits of trees, plants and other vegetation; humans cannot live without eating animals or plants. This is the basis upon which the material world operates. We have before us only two choices: either we eliminate the existence of the material world (which is without a doubt the essence of evil), or we accept the order of the world which encompasses the contradicting and conflicting interests of its beings each seeking its own completeness and perfection.

Conflict and contradiction are necessary, for in the material world you cannot dismantle them from each other. Think about it like even and odd numbers. For numbers like two and four, there must be pairs to add up to those numbers;

while odd numbers like 1 and 3, you need singles to add up to those numbers. You can't imagine the number four without a pair nor can you imagine three without the singularity. Similarly, if we were to suggest the elimination of contradiction and conflict then that would mean the demise of the material world. Therefore, the relative existence of evil does not harm the innovation of the creation of God and its exceptional order at all. In addition, it does not have an effect whatsoever on the design of existence in this world that came in the best of form and creation: "My Lord you did not create this in vain, glory be to You…"[9]

The Quality of Order

This idea is based on the concept that this world holds more good than it does evil. If you were to count all the good in the world and all the evil, you would be amazed with how much more good exists than evil. For this world to be neglected that would mean that the lot of good would be deserted for the little evil that is – that is not an outcome that the Wise would produce because it conflicts with wisdom itself. Wisdom dictates that pure good exists or that more good exists than relative evil, and this is the state of creation.

The Overlapping of Good and Evil

The more we grow and learn about the world around us, the more our outlook on things tends to change. Whenever we examine any issue, our background in education and experience has a big role in how broad or narrow our perspective is. On this basis, if we were to look at any of the things we

---

[9] Al-Haydari, *Al-Tawheed*, 2:294. Citing, Al-Tabatabaei, *Al-Mizan*, 11:339.

consider to have evil, we would realize that whatever evil we perceive is minor compared to all the good that it actually has. One of our scholars has been noted to have said, "These evils are only minimal and relative and are actually great benefits, for the more knowledgeable man becomes the greater his awareness is of the secrets of this world and the latent wisdom that it holds."[10]

What man may see as evil will become clearer to him as he contemplates and reflects that such evil has much more good for him than he once thought. Think of the trials and tribulations that all of humanity faces. The closer a person becomes to God the greater his tribulation will be. Imam Al-Sadiq (a) said, *"The people with the greatest tribulation are the prophets…"*[11]

Good is found in the depths of what could be perceived as evil and ease is found in the depths of what could be perceived as distress and hardship.

> *Did We not open your breast for you and relieve you of your burden which [almost] broke your back? Did We not exalt your name? Indeed ease accompanies hardship. Indeed ease accompanies hardship. So when you are done, appoint, and supplicate your Lord.*[12]

[10] Al-Yazdi, *Al-Manhaj Al-Jadeed fe Ta'leem Al-Falsafa*, 2:491.
[11] Al-Majlisi, *Bihar Al-Anwar*, 11:69.
[12] The Holy Quran. Chapter 94 [Arabic: *Al-Inshirah*]. Verses 1-8.

ASCRIBING
PARTNERS TO GOD

In the Name of God, the most Beneficent, the most Merciful

When Luqman said to his son, as he advised him: 'O my son! Do not ascribe any partners to God. Polytheism is indeed a great injustice.[1]

Oppression is an evil and abhorred thing. There is no reasonable person that would disagree with that. Rather, oppression is one of the greatest evils. The oppressor is not worthy of any praise. So we see that all social and political theories call for justice, no matter how different they may be. If oppression was a good thing, the oppressors would not deny it. The oppressor does not accept to be called so.

Oppression has a number of levels. The greatest level of oppression is to ascribe partners to God. The reasoning behind this conclusion lies in the fact that ascribing a partner to God is essentially a form of ungratefulness towards his infinite blessings that encompass both the believer and the nonbeliever. God says,

---

[1] The Holy Quran. Chapter 31 [Arabic: *Luqman*], Verse 13.

Whoever desires this transitory life, We expedite for him therein whatever We wish, for whomever We desire. Then We appoint hell for him, to enter it, blameful and spurned. Whoever desires the Hereafter and strives for it with an endeavor worthy of it, should he be faithful,—the endeavor of such will be well-appreciated. To these and to those—to all We extend the bounty of your Lord, and the bounty of your Lord is not confined.[2]

Similarly, in a supplication by Imam Sadeq (a) read after prayers in the month of Rajab, he calls unto God with the following: *"Oh You who grants His blessings to whomever asks Him. Oh You who grants His blessings to whomever does not ask Him and does not know Him, out of His compassion and mercy."*[3]

His blessings are never ending. They spring from His compassion and mercy towards His creations. Each of us enjoys countless blessings from Him at every moment of our lives. Reason dictates that we must be appreciative of such a benefactor. When all these blessings are met with ungratefulness towards this benefactor, it is a form of oppression. When the infinite blessings of God are met with ungratefulness, disbelief, and ascribing an associate to Him – that is the greatest form of oppression.

THE IMPORTANCE OF THIS TOPIC

Some may ask "what is the importance of discussing this topic? We Muslims all believe in God and do not ascribe

---

[2] The Holy Quran. Chapter 17 [The Ascension; Arabic: *Al-Israa*]. Verses 18-20.
[3] Ibn Tawuus. *Iqbaal Al-A'mal*, 3:211.

anything to Him. This type of topic should be targeted towards non-Muslims."

There are a number of reasons that call us to give special care to this topic. They include the following:

First, because mankind is a creation of God and is under His full control, and because the continuation of man's existence depends on His blessings, it behooves mankind to obey God in all His commands. Anything other than that is a declaration of rebellion against His command. The focal point of a person's existence must be God. *"Your Lord has decreed that you shall not worship anyone except Him...."*[4]

"Monotheism" is the most important notion for an individual on both a conceptual and a practical level. All of a person's actions and behaviors must be centered on the concept of monotheism. His intellectual base must be centered on the concept of monotheism. When a person begins to create other focal points in his life, there will be disharmony between the conceptual and practical aspects of his faith. This will cause a ripple effect, shaking the person's beliefs. In other words, a believer in God and His Oneness will undoubtedly have his belief reflect in all his actions and his daily routine. When he acts in any way that is incompatible with the concept of monotheism, there will be an inconsistency between the conceptual and the practical aspects of his faith. On a theoretical level, he will be a monotheistic believer in God. Yet, his actions are those of a disbeliever, and so he has practically ascribed a partner to God. This practical implication will, no doubt, have its effects on the

---

[4] The Holy Quran. Chapter 17 [The Ascension; Arabic: *Al-Israa*]. Verse 23.

individual's beliefs and he may begin to ascribe partners to God on a conceptual level as well, God forbid.

Second, when we hear of the concept of "ascribing a partner" to God, we automatically think of those polytheists that worshipped idols alongside Him, or those that worship his creations instead of Him. These are the most evident examples of ascribing a partner to God. However, the concept of ascribing partners is not limited to these examples. It has many other forms and levels which the Quran and the narrations have described and warned against. Therefore, we must learn about these forms of ascribing partners so that we can prevent ourselves from negligently falling into them and disobeying God in that way.

Third, ascribing a partner to God is one of the greatest of sins, and it is a sin that will not be forgiven if one does not repent from it. God says, *"Indeed God does not forgive that any partner should be ascribed to Him, but He forgives anything besides that to whomever He wishes. And whoever ascribes partners to God has certainly strayed into far error."*[5]

Even if all other sins may be forgiven through intercession or similar means, ascribing a partner to God is a sin that cannot be forgiven. No one can intercede for forgiveness of this sin. And even if one argues that this verse is addressing the highest stages of this sin, yet even the lowest stages are dangerous in that they might lead a person towards the higher stages of the sin. If a person begins to be degenerate in a small way at first, it will only be a matter of time before he falls into the greatest of sins. *"Then the fate of those who*

---

[5] The Holy Quran. Chapter 4 [The Women; Arabic: *Al-Nisaa*]. Verse 116.

*committed misdeeds was that they denied the signs of God and they
used to deride them.*"[6]

These points are enough to show us the importance of this
topic. True happiness in this world and the next depends
on it. The importance of the topic, along with the many
forms in which it can come and the unapparent nature of
some of those forms, allows it to pose a great danger on the
life of an individual in this world and in the hereafter.

SOME UNAPPARENT INSTANCES OF 'ASCRIBING PARTNERS'

We said that there are many levels and forms of ascribing
partners to God. In this chapter, we will shed light on some
of the unapparent instances of this deviance. Because the
apparent instances of ascribing partners to God are rarely
present within believing communities, we will not address
them here. The true danger lies in the unapparent instances
of ascribing partners, which are found more profusely in believing communities. God says, "*And most of them do not believe
in God without ascribing partners to Him.*"[7]

Ascribing a Partner in Obedience

God gives us an example of this in the Quran; He says,
"*They have taken their scribes and their monks as lords besides God,
and also Christ, Mary's son; though they were commanded to worship
only the One God, there is no god except Him; He is far too immaculate to have any partners that they ascribe [to Him]!*"[8] The verse

---

6 The Holy Quran. Chapter 30 [The Romans; Arabic: *Al-Room*]. Verse 10.
7 The Holy Quran. Chapter 12 [Arabic: *Yusuf*]. Verse 106.
8 The Holy Quran. Chapter 9 [The Repentance; Arabic: *Al-Tawba*]. Verse 31.

clearly indicates that there are some who took priests and monks as gods rather than God. They worshiped them instead of God. When referring back to the narrations that explain this verse, we find that they point to an important truth. Our narrations tell us that these people that are addressed in the verse did not actually perform typical acts of worship for their priests and monks. Rather, they used to obey them to the point of worship. It is narrated that one of the companions of Imam Sadiq (a) asked him about this verse, so he replied *"By God, these [priests and monks] did not call the people to worship them, and if they had people would not have worshipped them. Rather, they gave a verdict making that which is impermissible permissible and that which is permissible impermissible. In that way, they worshipped them without realizing it."*[9] This allows us to make a number of remarks:

First, ascribing partners to God can come from an environment of faith and worship. It's not that a person ascribes partners to God only after living with the corrupt and deviant and taking from their ways. A person can fall into this great deviance while he lives a life that appears as a life of faith, worship, and piety. Therefore, it is imperative on every individual to reflect on his actions at all times, as he does not know when he might fall into the trap of this deviation.

Second, each individual, as a servant of God, must give complete obedience to Him and everyone that He gave authority. Other than that, obedience should not be given to anyone, unless if it was somehow linked to the obedience of God. Even if a person is of the best of the worshippers of God, you have no reason to obey him unless his commands

---

[9] Al-Kulayni, *Al-Kafi*, 1:53.

fall in line with the commands of God. Monks and priests were the scholars in God's way, and so they represented a prime example. The verse was not meant to distinguish monks and priests as a category; rather the concept applies at all levels. Be it clergy or non-clergy, Muslims or not, obedience should not be given to anyone if that obedience does not fall in line with obedience of God. If obedience of clergy goes against God's command, then that obedience is a form of ascribing partners to God.

This is why we see that the school of thought of the Household of the Prophet (a) emphasizes justice and piety in a scholar. A scholar may have abundant knowledge from books, but without commitment to the faith in action, that scholar is unqualified to be even a leader of congregational prayer – let alone a religious authority. Only when a scholar is just, committed to the faith in action, can he be followed in matters of religion. Of course, there are also other conditions such as being the most learned amongst the scholars if the scholars disagree. The school of thought of the Household of the Prophet (a) emphasizes that knowledge alone does not suffice in a scholar; rather he must be committed to the faith in actions, in obedience to God Almighty, as well. This can be seen in a narration of Imam Hassan al-Askari (a) where he quotes Imam Sadeq (a) as saying, "...*as for those of the scholars who has safeguarded himself and maintained his religion, who acts contrary to his desires and obeys the command of his Lord, then the laymen may emulate him...*"[10]

If we cannot obey the highest scholars, who are the objects of religious emulation, without first confirming that they are

---

[10] Al-Tabrasi, *Al-Ihtijaj*, 2:263.

pious and just, then what say you of obeying other religious figure without making a similar confirmation? But even if we confirm that such religious figures are pious, we may not be justified in following their personal opinions because they may not have the expertise that qualifies them! Sure, if they encourage us to do something that we already know God commands or if they discourage us from something that we already know God forbids, that is a different story. Similarly, if we gain sure confidence that they are merely re-laying the expert opinions of the highest scholars, then that is also a different story. We must learn matters of faith only from the most trusted of sources. Even in the most simple of matters, we do not follow just anyone in everything they say; rather, we take their opinion seriously only after we have assurance of their honesty and reliability. How can we, then, take matters of our faith from just anyone without first confirming his knowledge and his piety?

Third, justice is an important concept that must continue to be a focal point everywhere in the world. That is why every individual must keep the person from whom he learns about his religion under close watch, being careful that he does not deviate from the path. Each individual must take it upon himself to follow the leadership of religious figures only so long as they remain in obedience to God and guide to His path. If any religious figure is to deviate from the path, he becomes no longer worthy of leadership. If we were to simply follow religious figures without applying the standards of piety and knowledge, then we may ultimately be led to follow corrupt and unqualified religious figures. The verse mentioned earlier addresses people who knew of their priests' deviance and still followed them, and that is how they moved themselves from the safety of monotheism to the corruption of ascribing a partner to God. Faith is the dearest thing to mankind. No man, no matter how high and mighty he may be, is worth my sacrificing my religion for him. We seek a connection with scholars so long as they are connected to God, and so long as they are representing to us and following the model of the Holy Prophet (s) and his Household (a).

We also live at a time of deviance, and we see many claims and theories being passed around by all sorts of individuals. It is important to be careful with such claims. We must handle them as keen observers. This is especially true for any claim that concerns our Twelfth Holy Imam (atfs); these especially require the utmost care and alertness. In these matters, we must refer back to the knowledgeable scholars and continue to discuss critically and seek to understand the truth of the matter concerning the Imam of the Time (atfs). Becoming completely blind followers of any claim will only lead to regret.

Ascribing a Partner in Intent

Another type of ascribing a partner to God comes through insincerity in intent. This form is very dangerous and we have been specifically warned against it by the Quran and the narrations. It is even given a name – *Riyaa'*, that is insincerity, showing off or duplicity. This is a sin that invalidates all of a person's worship and draws him to the trap of ascribing partners to God. Simply, duplicity in worship occurs when a person attempts to deceive others by pretending to be a holy and religious person. Such a person would perform his prayers in the best of manners in public and he would take his time in performing it. At the same time, he would not care to pray when he is in private, or he would pray quickly and incompletely. Why would anyone do this? Some may do this so they can attract attention, or to gain social status, or for some other worldly reason.

Worship is a duty owed to God and no one else – that is one of the meanings of monotheism. This also means that we cannot worship anyone but Him or let anything else enter and corrupt the sincere intention of worshipping Him. A person who practices duplicity has broken this cardinal rule. He worships not for the sake of God, but for the attention. Or maybe he worships God for his sake, but also to gain a higher social status. This duplicity is essentially ascribing a partner to God in intent.

The Quran and the narrations have warned us of the severe implications of duplicity. They tell us that duplicity is a characteristic of the hypocrites and the disbelievers. God says in the Quran, *"And those who spend their wealth to be seen by people, and believe neither in God nor in the Last Day. As for him who has Satan for his companion—an evil companion is he!"*[11] The Quran also asserts, *"The hypocrites indeed seek to deceive God, but it is He who outwits them. When they stand up for prayer, they stand up lazily, showing off to the people and not remembering God except a little."*[12]

A believer should never intend anything other than closeness to God when he is performing any worship. Duplicity and insincerity in intent would only lead to the loss of the

[11] The Holy Quran. Chapter 4 [The Women; Arabic: *Al-Nisaa*]. Verse 38.
[12] Ibid, Verse 142.

work and meriting of punishment in the hereafter. It is narrated that Imam Sadiq (a) once told Abbad bin Katheer when he saw him in the mosque, *"Woe to you, Oh Abbad! Beware of duplicity. Whoever works for anyone but God, God will forsake them to seek refuge in whoever they worked for."*[13]

It is also narrated that he (a) said, *"Every instance of duplicity is ascribing a partner to God. Whoever works for the sake of people, his rewards will be from the people. Whoever works for the sake of God, his rewards will be from God."*[14] There are many other narrations in this regard.

No one should think that they are immune from falling into the trap of duplicity. We sometimes live in a state of heedlessness even towards our own actions and intention. We begin to act without any deliberation, sometimes even mindlessly. Therefore, we must always be attentive to what our true intentions are. We must make sure that we are truly sincere to God. We must make sure that this sincerity is present before, throughout, and after every action that we take. Sometimes we begin to do something with a sincere intention, but we find later on that our intention had shifted so that it is no longer sincerely and solely directed towards God. That is why our Immaculate Imams (a) have taught us the importance of maintaining your deeds through sincerity of intention. Imam Baqir (a) said,

> *Maintaining a deed is harder than performing it... A man may connect to a relative and spend something for the sake of God – the One who has no partner – and it will be written for him as a secret [act]. He would mention it [to some-*

---

[13] Al-Kulayni, *Al-Kafi*, 2:222.
[14] Ibid.

one], so it would be erased and written again as a public [act]. Then he would mention it [to someone else], so it would be erased and written down as [an act of] duplicity.[15]

So working for the sake of God must be done in complete sincerity. Having any sort of duplicity in the action will be a cause for that deed's annulment. It is narrated that the Prophet (s) said, *"God does not accept any act that has an atom's worth of duplicity."*[16]

Ascribing a Partner through Heresy

God, as the creator of mankind, wants us to be sincere to him in all aspects. And because God alone has the right to set religious teachings, and because religion is something that is meant for Him, any form of heresy is considered as ascribing a partner to Him. It is not for us to formulate opinions and thoughts and ascribe them to God. God is more glorious than we can imagine, and we cannot impose our own flawed opinions unto Him. It can be a great trage-dy when a person falls into this without even realizing it. Whatever innovation or opinion, if ascribed to God, is here-sy, even if the intention behind it was worship or good. It is a form of ascribing a partner to God because the individual is putting his opinion alongside God's commands and treat-ing them equally. We cannot choose the way in which we wish to worship; we must worship God the way He wants to be worshipped.

Suppose that an individual wanted to worship God by fast-ing from sunset to sunrise, or to pray five *raka'at* instead of

---

[15] Ibid.

[16] Al-Majlisi, *Bihar Al-Anwar*, 69:304.

four in one of the daily prayers. Even if this might appear to be a form of worship, it is in reality a transgression against the boundaries and laws drawn for us by God. Worship consists of obedience to the Lord's commands. We cannot act as divine legislators in His stead.

OTHER APPLICATIONS

The traditions also point out to a form of ascribing a partner to God that may be even less apparent than the form described above. When a person adopts an opinion and an ideology and makes it the standard of his interaction with others, in conflict with God's commands, he has ascribed a partner to God. In a narration of Imam Baqir (a), he was asked about the least form of ascribing a partner to God. The Imam (a) replied, "[The state of one who would] *say that the pit [of a date] is a pebble and that the pebble is a pit [of a date], and take that as his religion.*"[17] To attribute a false notion to God and consider it part of God's religion sprouts from obedience to satanic humans or demons, or one's own lowly desires instead of obedience to God Almighty. Thus, it is a form of ascribing partners to God.[18]

In a similar narration, a man asks Imam Sadeq (a) the same question. The Imam (a) replies, "[The state of one] *who innovates an opinion, then he would love others according to [their conformity to] that opinion or hate them according to [their conformity to] that opinion.*"[19] An innovated opinion is one with no legitimate religious basis, regardless whether it is related to the princi-

---

[17] Al-Kulayni, *Al-Kafi*, 2:397.

[18] Al-Majlisi, *Mir'at al-'uqul fi Sharḥ Akhbar 'al al-Rasul*, 11:174.

[19] Al-Kulayni, *Al-Kafi*, 2:397.

ples of faith or the branches of faith. This is a form of ascribing a partner to God, because it would be tantamount to taking a Lord besides God Almighty.[20] The opinion may be wrong and thus God may want us to love instead of hate or hate instead of love, depending on the truth. Love and hate should be for the sake of God alone and must be according to the standards of God alone.

There are many more forms of ascribing a partner to God. For example, if we believe that our sustenance comes independently from human beings, or that the doctor has the independent ability to cure, or that any action is undertaken independently by the actor. Yes, if we give them these descriptions with the idea that they are dependent on God and are only tools through which God provides His blessings, then it we would not be ascribing any partner to Him. We must realize that He alone is the ultimate Sustainer, the Healer, the Giver, the All-Merciful, and the possessor of all the other divine attributes. Anyone else that may do us any service is only a medium through which God delivers His blessings. That is why Imam Sadiq (a) is reported to have said in describing how an individual may ascribe a partner to God,

> *[Imam Sadiq (a) said]* ... "It is when a man says 'without so and so I would have perished,' 'without so and so, such and such would have happened to me,' or 'without so and so my family would have been lost.' Do you not see that he has ascribed a partner to God in His kingdom, blessing him and driving off evil from him." *[The narrator*

---

[20] Al-Majlisi, *Mir'at al-'uqul fi Sharḥ Akhbar 'al al-Rasul*, 11:174.

then] asked, "what about saying 'if God had not blessed me with so and so, I would have perished'?" The Imam (a) replied, "Yes, there's nothing wrong with that.*"[21]*

We must always be wary not to fall into the traps of Satan. A person may fall into one of the many snares of ascribing a partner to God, especially since many of its forms are not readily recognizable. But with sincerity in turning to God Almighty, all difficulties can be overcome, and only blessings and bliss await us, God-willing.

We ask Him to make us immune of deviance, heedlessness, and ascribing partners to Him, He is surely the All-Listening, the All-Answering.

---

[21] Al-Majlisi, *Bihar Al-Anwar*, 69:100.

THE FINAL REVELATION

In the Name of God, the most Beneficent, the most Merciful

Mankind were a single community; then God sent the prophets as bearers of good news and warners, and He sent down with them the Book with the truth, that it may judge between the people concerning that about which they differed, and none differed in it except those who had been given it, after the manifest proofs had come to them, out of envy among themselves. Then God guided those who had faith to the truth of what they differed in, by His will, and God guides whomever He wishes to a straight path.[1]

THE NECESSITY OF PROPHETHOOD

God made creation of two types. The first type of creatures has no free will. Rather these creatures are subject to a system of being and behavior that they cannot deviate from. This is the case with most living creatures that have their own set system for feeding, reproduction, habitation, etc. A seed will grow as dictated by the laws of nature that God

---

[1] The Holy Quran. Chapter 2 [The Cow; Arabic: *Al-Baqara*]. Verse 213.

has drawn for it. The same is true with other objects, such as the sun, planets, and animals.

The second type of creatures is not subject to the dictates of natural behavioral patterns; rather they have the free will to change their thoughts and behaviors. This is seen most evidently in humankind, which possesses abilities that are not found in other creatures on this Earth; that is, freedom of choice. Each human being has the ability to make choices and adopt life goals that he will work to achieve. We are not subjected to one path in our life that we cannot deviate from; And because mankind has the freedom of choice and has goals and ambitions, there must be processes and laws put in place to govern how each individual works towards those goals. But because each individual has his own goals and ambitions, it is normal for each to prefer a set of laws and institutions that best serve his own personal, family, or class interests. This is why we see a contradiction between our personal goals and the collective goals of communities and nations. This is a major cause for conflict between mankind. This may be why the angels professed their concern when God first decided to create humanity, asking *"Will You set in it someone who will cause corruption in it and shed blood, while we celebrate Your praise and proclaim Your sanctity?"*[2]

God is the All-Wise creator of mankind and he has boundless mercy and compassion toward us. His infinite wisdom and mercy dictate that He provides mankind with a solution for this constant struggle between individualistic and communal goals and ambitions. This solution was delivered to us by the prophets that He has sent. The solution that God

---

[2] Ibid, Verse 30.

has provided resolves the issue of these conflicting ambitions.

But why did God choose the prophets as the means for delivering this solution?

The main purpose behind the system that was set for mankind is to nurture and educate us about the hereafter and that all of our ambitions can be achieved therein if we would only compromise on the ambitions of this world. And because the hereafter is of the unseen world beyond, we need special guidance to direct us to its existence and the path that we must take to reach it. It cannot be reached without disciplining the self in accordance with divine commands. This special divine guidance that we need is manifested in the prophets.

God did not create mankind and leave us without a system that would guide our actions. If that were the case, our creation on this Earth would be futile and frivolous, and God the All-Wise is Exalted beyond such description. We cannot imagine that God would create us with a purpose and yet not give us a means to fulfill that purpose – "*I did not create the jinn and the humans except that they may worship Me.*"[3].

Therefore, it is only natural that God creates a system of teachings and legislation that will lead us to our ultimate goal. Yet, there must still be someone to deliver those teachings and implement this legislation. This individual must possess two characteristics: a spiritual state that allows him to connect to the upper realms, and a human character that allows him to live with mankind as part of them.

---

[3] The Holy Quran. Chapter 51 [Arabic: *Al-Dhariyat*]. Verse 56.

These characters are manifested in the individuals that reached the status of prophethood. These individuals did not differ from the rest of us in their humanity. Yet, because of their nurturement, their discipline, their circumstances, their exercise of free will and divine blessings, they are given the ability to communicate with the upper realms and receive divine revelation. They would carry the Lord's message and lead humanity to the shores of salvation.

THE PROGRESSION OF THE MESSAGE

One may ask "why did God send all these messengers with different religions? Why did He not send one messenger with a single message to be implemented throughout time?"

There is no doubt that the essence of the divine message did not change from the time of the first messenger of God to the last of His prophets.

The essence of the divine message is complete servitude to God. Mankind is limited and is bound to obey others. That obedience can either be directed to God, or it can be directed to Satan and his kind or to the self and its desires. Obedience to anyone but god is considered obedience to "false deities." God says:

> God is the [ally] of the faithful: He brings them out of
> darkness into light. As for the faithless, their [allies] are the
> fake deities, who drive them out of light into darkness. They
> shall be the inmates of the Fire, and they will remain in it
> [forever].[4]

---

[4] The Holy Quran. Chapter 2 [The Cow; Arabic: Al-Baqara]. Verse 257.

All of the divine messages were targeted toward this purpose; to provide mankind with the means to reach the goal for which they were created and placed on this Earth – "*I did not create the jinn and the humans except that they may worship Me.*"[5]

It is also evident that mankind did not always possess the same intellectual capacities across the millennia. Mankind is in a state of constant progression. We have developed from primitive cavemen in the Stone Age to the Bronze Age and then to the Iron Age, and so on. Some even suggest that we have been evolving physiologically as well as intellectually, but we will not delve into that discussion. What is important is that the progression and development of humanity is an evident reality. This makes sense because mankind did not have any experience at the beginning of its journey. Each age accumulates and builds upon the experiences of past ages and civilizations. The capacity of humans throughout these different stages differed and, therefore, it makes sense that the details of the message given to Noah (a) would not differ from the details of the message given to Abraham (a), and from the details of the message given to Moses (a), and so on.

At mankind's early stages, life was not complicated by society and civilization. But the further that humanity progressed, the more issues and conflicts arose for mankind. At each stage of mankind's development, the prophets were sent with a message befitting the issues of the time. Progression in the divine message is a necessity for mankind, and God in His wisdom responded to this need. All of these messages

---

[5] The Holy Quran. Chapter 51 [Arabic: *Al-Dhariyat*]. Verse 56.

are one in their essence; they all call for monotheistic belief in God, full servitude to Him, and virtue in morality and character. But this one essence does not necessitate that all facets of the message be the same, rather *"For each [community] among you We had appointed a code [of law] and a path, and had God wished He would have made you one community, but [His purposes required] that He should test you in respect to what He has given you."*[6]

WHY WAS THE PROPHET (S) THE LAST MESSENGER

The last stage of progression in the divine message was the stage of the message of Islam. It was first delivered at a time and place of utmost failure in intellect, society, and politics. That was embodied in the community of Hijaz in the Arabian Peninsula. Even though some places on the peninsula saw some advancement in civilization at that time, such as the nearby kingdom of Yemen, Hijaz did not earn any share in that advancement.

Intellectually, the people of Hijaz were idol worshipping pagans. They were ignorant and illiterate, except for a few. Socially, they did not possess any values that protected society from degeneracy. A man used to inherit his father's harem and practice with them what his father had practiced. Women at that time were in the most misfortunate situation; they were either buried alive or faced the more misfortunate life in such a community. Politically, Hijaz did not possess the stature of a sovereign nation. Anarchy reigned during that time. Survival was for the most powerful. Theft and exploi-

---

[6] The Holy Quran. Chapter 5 [The Banquet; Arabic: *Al-Maeda*]. Verse 48.

tation was seen as a source of prestige. This was one of the vilest examples of human civilization.

The Prophet Muhammad was sent to this community to spread the divine message. He had the task of delivering a profound message in such difficult circumstances. Overall, humankind had reached a stage of intellectual progression that allowed them to receive God's greatest message. This message came to guide humanity through the last stage of its journey in this world. It contained a number of characteristics that made it unique compared to all the previous messages. These unique characteristics include the following:

1. The message of Islam is far more expansive than all the others. It came with a system of legislation that encompassed many aspects of life. For each stage of life, there are laws, etiquettes, and traditions that the individual must follow. Some of these laws are binding, while the others are advisory. Whoever abides by these advisory laws will be rewarded and will find great guidance in them. We do not find any other message that contains such a detailed code of conduct.

2. The message of Islam is also very effective in changing the individual when applied. It changed a community that lived in a state close to that of beasts to one of the most advanced civilizations on Earth. Instead of simply worrying about their debasing desires, they began to carry out the divine message of Islam. Their goal became to free themselves from

the servitude of the self and the desires to reach the freedom of servitude to God.

3. The message of Islam also brought a unique social order to the world. If we take a closer look at history, we will find that some of the social values that the Quran taught were only adopted by other societies hundreds of years after the birth of Islam. Islam taught social cohesion and fought all forms of tyranny at a time when lacking such values was corrupting the world.

These distinctions made the message of Prophet Muhammad (s) unique and gave it the ability to adapt to different circumstances and times. Still, there are a number of questions that must be answered about the nature of Islam and why it is the last of the divine messages.

WAS ISLAM SAFEGUARDED FROM DISTORTIONS?

We know that the messages that previous messengers had carried were distorted by some of their followers as time passed on. That's natural, as the further people grow away from the time of revelation, some distortion will happen because of misunderstanding and inaccurate mediums. Some may even intentionally attempt to distort the religion to fit their own desires. That is why God would send a prophet from time to time to purify the religion from whatever distortions may have occurred as well as deliver different codes of law suitable for humanity at that stage.

The Islamic community is not immune from these causes, as it is as much a human society as those before it were. Why does God not send more prophets to correct whatever deviations that may have occurred in Islam? There are two primary answers that are proposed by Muslim scholars.

The Muslim Community as the Safeguard

One group of scholars have argued that Islam is a complete and comprehensive religion and that the Prophet (s) was able to nurture a virtuous community that was able to preserve the values and laws that it was given. Thus, based on this theory, the Muslim community is the one safeguarding the message of Islam. The Prophet (s) left a Muslim community that was mature enough to choose its own path and establish a political order that was able to preserve the Quran and the message of Islam.

And before discussing this view, let us first make the following point. Preservation of Islam goes back to the preservation of the Quran as the source of Islamic teachings. The Quran was safeguarded from distortion as a text by God – *"Indeed We have sent down the Reminder, and indeed We will preserve it."*[7]

The Muslim community did not play the role of safeguard towards the Quran and its teachings. Although the Muslim community held fast to many of the teachings of Islam in the years following the passing of the Prophet (s), but that was due to the fact that most people then had fresh memories of the Prophet (s) and his teachings. The Muslim nation soon began to deviate. With the rise of the Umayyads and the Abbasids to power, religion became a tool in the hands of the tyrants. Preservation of the Quran as a text goes back

---

[7] The Holy Quran. Chapter 15 [Arabic: *Al-Hijr*]. Verse 9.

to the promise that God made in the verse.[8] Because these two dynasties could not distort the text of the Quran, they began to distort people's understanding of it through distorting its exegesis. The traditions of the Prophet (s) faced a worse fate, as the nation did not preserve the text of his teachings, but began to misrepresent, falsify, and fabricate according to their desires and the desires of the tyrants in power. The Muslim community certainly did not play the role of the safeguard of Islam and its teachings.

The Household of the Prophet as the Safeguards of the Message

The second theory states that although God sent to us a complete message that is Islam, He did not leave the Muslim community without guidance after the completion of the message and after the death of the Prophet (s). God did not leave Muslims to their own devices. Instead, He allowed for a number of devout individuals to inherit His vicegerency and be the guides to everything that relates to this world or the next.

What ended with the death of the Prophet (s) was divine revelation. However, these vicegerents hold the same position of guidance as the Prophet (s). They are the ones who protect the message and teachings of the Prophet (s). They share the same status with a number of prophets such as Prophet Abraham (a); the Quran relates the following conversation between God and Abraham (a) *"[God] said, 'I am making you the Imam of mankind.' Said he, 'And from among my descendants?' He said, 'My pledge does not extend to the unjust.'"*[9]

---

[8] Ibid.
[9] The Holy Quran. Chapter 2 [The Cow; Arabic: *Al-Baqara*]. Verse 124.

The Prophet (s) delivered the message and guided and nurtured the Muslims to abide by its teachings. But after the death of the Prophet (s) and the expansion and progression of the Muslim community, there were some questions that were not readily answered by the Quran or the traditions of the Prophet (s).

This is why we believe that the Prophet (s) gave his knowledge and understanding of the divine message to those who could step into the position of guidance after him. This is what Imam Baqir (a) refers to in the narration:

> *We inherit perfection and completeness that God brought down on His Prophet (s) in the verse:* "Today I have perfected your religion for you, and I have completed My blessing upon you, and I have approved Islam as your religion." *The Earth will not be empty of those who complete these matters that others fall short of.*[10]

This is in addition to the fact that the Holy Quran, which is the guiding constitution for all Muslims, has some verses that are summations while others are specific. Some of its verses are ambiguous while some are unambiguous. Some of its verses are absolute while others are restricted. Some of its verses are abrogating and others are abrogated. The Muslims differed in their opinions and split into many sects due to their lack of knowledge in some of these matters and differences in exegesis. There must have been someone to go back to. The reference point must be an individual with a comprehensive understanding of Quranic teachings and divine legislation. Only such an individual would be able to

---

[10] Al-Majlisi, *Bihar Al-Anwar*, 46:307.

solve the debates between Muslims in regards to Quranic teachings and divine law. These individuals are no other than the Holy Household of the Prophet (s). They are those who stick to the Quran, the ones who drank from the pure source of knowledge that is the Prophet (s). They took a scoop from the generous seas of the Prophet's (s) wisdom and safeguarded it in the most pure of vessels in their spacious hearts. That is why the Prophet (s) described them as follows, "*I leave amongst you two weighty things, the Book of God and my household. They will not separate until they reach me at the Pond [of Paradise].*"[11]

If we were to study the lives of these great individuals, we would find that they fulfilled this role to its utmost extent. The fact that the Muslim nation deviated from their path did not stop them from spreading their knowledge and teaching about the divine message. They stood in the face of anyone who would try to distort the teachings and legislation of Islam. They stood patient in spite of all that they faced while they fulfilled this duty.

They were the highest voice for truth and a sturdy wall in the face of the axes of deviance that attempted to destroy Islam. They were truthful exegetes of the Quran that the Muslim nation could not understand its ingenious and precise meanings. This divine vicegerency still stands with the Imam of The Time (a) who will make himself known when the time is right to fill the Earth with justice and equity just as it has been filled with injustice and transgression. He will return everything to its place and remove every flaw and deviance that has been attributed to Islam. He will rebuke all

---

[11] Al-Nisabouri, *Al-Mustadrak*, 3:148.

the additions that have been added to the divine legislation and restore all that has been lost from it. While we currently do not have direct access to the immaculate Imam (a), we do have access to those whom he referred us to – the qualified, upright expert jurists. Humanity may not be ready for the Imam (a)'s leadership yet. Moreover, oppressors may be the key hindrance stopping the Imam (a) from making himself known. Furthermore, the Imam's (a) own followers may not be living up to the standards required for the Imam's (a) sacred mission. Whatever the Divine Wisdom may be, until the Imam (a) makes himself known, this situation in which we refer to the expert, pious scholars, preparing for the Imam (a), is the next best solution.

This is how God has preserved the message of Islam from distortion.

IS ISLAM TOO RIGID?

So Islam is the last of the divine messages. Whatever the teachings of Islam are, they will stand as such until the end of times. *"The [issue deemed to be] halal (permissible) [in the law] of Muhammad (s) is halal until the Day of Judgment, and the [issue deemed to be] haram (forbidden) [in the law] of Muhammad (s) is haram until the Day of Judgment."*[12] But doesn't that imply that Islam is too rigid since it cannot change from the days of revelation until the Day of Judgment?

The change in nature and the materialistic world does not necessitate change in the constant standards, values, and principles. The material world changes constantly. But does

---

[12] Al-Kulayni, *Al-Kafi*, 1:57.

this change encompass mathematical equations and laws? Even though these laws apply to the material world, they remain constant. The same is true with the laws and standards of the metaphysical. The laws of Islam were set to guide humanity in its journey towards what God has wished for it. These laws are not affected by the material changes of this world.

But what about the change and progression within human society? These changes are driven social dynamics and other factors. If the primary driving force was the innate nature of mankind, the results will be constant because that nature is constant. So, for example, the sexual drive that is built in mankind's instincts is needed for reproduction and continuation of society. The innate nature of mankind will lead it to marriage and the creation of households. This social phenomenon remains constant and is governed by the constant laws of religion.

DOES ISLAM NEED TO BE REFORMED?

One may posit the following:

As we mentioned before, humanity is in constant progression on an intellectual and civil level. We have seen developments in many fields since the revelation of the message of Islam, and many of them cannot be readily addressed by religious texts. So for example, while Islam came to govern the simple economic realities of 14 centuries past, it cannot readily govern the complex economic structures of today. The same is true for the social and political developments in human society.

Before answering this misconception, let us discuss two premises for our answer.

First, there are a number of fundamental constants in human life that have not changed and will not change through time. This is due either to the fact that the constant stems from human instincts or because it is part of the innate nature of mankind. Examples of these constants include the following:

Worship. The need for an individual to engage in worship is of the innate nature of the individual, as each of us feels the need to belong to a greater power; a greater power that is omnipotent and omniscient. This innate instinct needs to be structured in a system of worship so as to protect from deviances. So because the subject performing worship (the human) is constant, the laws of worship must also be constant from the time of the Prophet (s) to today. There are real benefits to be gained from the legislation. So long as the subject matter of the legislation (in this case, the human) is the same where it counts, since the time of the Prophet (s) until today, the same benefit of worship still exists. Therefore, given that no clash of other binding issues come into play, the same rules regarding worship apply.

Family. The familial connection, such as that between father and son or between brothers, is natural and creates a spiritual connection and kinship between individuals. These relationships require laws to govern them, starting at their daily interactions to laws of marriage and inheritance. And just as these relationships remain constant at all times, so too the laws that govern them remain constant.

Morality. Morality is given a great importance within Islamic teachings. Islam set laws that deal with crimes such as fornication, theft, gambling, and other morally reprehensible acts. This is either due to the great damage that such immorality deals to society or because of the inherent reprehensibility of it on its own merit. And because the harms or inherent reprehensibility of these acts are constant, so too must the laws that deal with them be constant.

Therefore, so long as the subject to which the legislation applies remains constant, so too the legislation will remain constant.

Second, in addition to these constants that exist in human society, there are circumstances that change with the change of the time and place. They are in constant change, and they drive the change of humanity's advancement. The laws that deal with these changing circumstances must be dynamic. However, they must be at all times in harmony with the constant laws that deal with the static aspects of human life. If we were to assume that any group of unqualified individuals from mankind is free to change these laws as it sees fit, it would surely create laws that are inharmonious with the constant laws we spoke of above. People will begin to change religion to what aligns with their own whimsical desires. Humanity must objectively reach a set of laws that are at all times harmonious and consistent. That would be the sensible thing to do. This is why this task was given to the specialists – the *Mujtahidoun*, or jurists, that have spent their life seeking to understand the intricacies of Islam's teachings and divine law.

So for example, there is a general and constant law that God dictated in the verse: *"Do not eat up your wealth among yourselves wrongfully...."*[13]

Based on that, we see that our scholars derived a number of transactional rulings, such as the impermissibility of buying and selling blood or human waste. The reasoning behind these rulings is that there is no benefit that can be derived from these things; if someone is selling them they are receiving something of value and giving nothing of value, and are thus taking others' wealth wrongfully. However, with technological advances, we have found a great use for blood and we can now use it to save lives. When this advancement happened, the transaction on blood was removed from the general law. That is why some of our contemporary scholars have ruled that it is permissible to sell blood.

In addition to this, we see that there are a number of things that Islamic law took a neutral stance towards. There are a number of issues that are advanced by Islamic teachings, such as education, charity, and defense of the self and others. However, Islam did not dictate how these things are to be implemented. Islam places great importance on knowledge and education, but leaves the mode of education for society to determine. Islam did not require anyone to attend a class about reading a book or vice versa; rather it allowed each individual and the community as a whole to determine how knowledge will be spread and to use all the means necessary in that regard, so long as there is no conflict with any of Islam's general laws.

---

[13] The Holy Quran. Chapter 2 [The Cow; Arabic: *Al-Baqara*]. Verse 188.

THE MEANS OF SALVATION

In the Name of God, the most Beneficent, the most Merciful

O you who have faith! Be wary of God, and seek the means of recourse to Him, and wage jihad in His way, so that you may be felicitous.[1]

The Grand Prophet Muhammad (s) is the master of all creation. Who can give justice to the character of the man who God described with the verse, *"and indeed you possess a great character"*[2]? God also says *"We did not send you but as a mercy to all the nations."*[3]

Who can claim that they can do justice to the characteristics traits of this prophet, the prophet who God has made the greatest of the most honorable of His creations? No one else has ever reached his status. He is the one who *"drew nearer and nearer [to God] until he was within two bows' length or even nearer."*[4]

---

[1] The Holy Quran. Chapter 5 [The Banquet; Arabic: *Al-Maeda*]. Verse 35.

[2] The Holy Quran. Chapter 68 [The Pen; Arabic: *Al-Qalam*]. Verse 4.

[3] The Holy Quran. Chapter 21 [The Prophets; Arabic: *Al-Anbiya'*]. Verse 107.

[4] The Holy Quran. Chapter 53 [The Star; Arabic: *Al-Najm*]. Verses 8, 9.

The Prophet (s) passed away after spending his life in the sake of spreading the message of God. It is the message that, if humanity would have adopted, would have delivered us from all weakness, cruelty, war, deviance, and oppression. The Prophet (s) left this worldly life after facing much harm and oppression from his own people – he himself has said *"no prophet has been harmed as much as I have been harmed."*[5] With his death, humanity lost its truest leader.

No one can do justice to his character. We realize our shortcoming in this matter. Still, we find it imperative that we attempt to describe some of the most important of his characteristics below.

THE NAME OF GOD AND THE NAME OF THE PROPHET

In order to highlight the greatness of the Prophet (s) and his stature, we find that God has coupled His great name with the name of his prophet on many occasions. Furthermore, God has commanded us to deal with the Prophet (s) in the same way we would deal with God whenever the names are coupled.

For example, God coupled obedience to God with obedience of the Prophet (s). God says *"Whoever obeys the Apostle certainly obeys God; and as for those who turn their backs [on you]; We have not sent you to keep watch over them."*[6] By God's own words, obedience to the Prophet (s) is obedience to God. This is proof that the Prophet (s) has no wish or desire that

---

[5] Al-Majlisi, *Bihar Al-Anwar*, 39:56.
[6] The Holy Quran. Chapter 4 [The Women; Arabic: *Al-Nisaa*]. Verse 80.

is in conflict with the will of God. This is due to his great stature and his closeness to God. God chose him as the medium to deliver the message because God knew that he would exercise his free will to please God and would be more worthy than all others. Hence, God supported him and protected him from all types of error. We cannot imagine that the Prophet (s) would want anything that God may dislike. Everything that he does is exactly as God wants. This is why God made obedience to the Prophet (s) an act of obedience to God Himself.

God has also established that allegiance to the Prophet (s) is a cause for His love. God Says, *"Say, 'If you love God, then follow me; God will love you and forgive you your sins, and God is all-forgiving, all-merciful.'"*[7] So obedience to the Prophet (s) and following his guidance is a means for attaining the love of God. The Prophet (s)every action or lack thereof is guidance, and, thus, a means and a path towards God.

God has also sworn by the very life of Prophet Muhammad (s), an honor that God has not given to any other person in the holy Qur'an, pointing to the distinct significance of the Prophet's role as a guide in life. God says, *"By your life, they were bewildered in their drunkenness."*[8] The fact that God swears by any of His creatures is an indication of the significance of that creature. God has sworn by a number of His creatures, such as the sun, the moon, the dawn, the stars, and other creations. However, He never swore by the life of any of his creatures in the holy Qur'an other than by the life of the Holy Prophet (s). This directs attention to the significance

---

[7] The Holy Quran. Chapter 3 [Arabic: *Aal Imran*]. Verse 31.
[8] The Holy Quran. Chapter 15 [Arabic: *Al-Hijr*]. Verse 72.

of the life of this final prophet who is the lamp of guidance and the guide to the straight path.[9]

God has also given the Prophet (s) the ability to see the acts of all creations by the will of God. God says:

> *They will offer you excuses when you return to them. Say, 'Do not make excuses; we will never believe you. God has informed us of your state of affairs. God and His Apostle will observe your conduct, then you will be returned to the Knower of the sensible and the Unseen, and He will inform you concerning what you used to do.'*[10]

There are also other verses and traditions that confirm this. This is the greatest of honors. God has coupled the name of the Prophet (s) with His name. God gave the Prophet (s) the ability to monitor the deeds of His creatures. God gave the Prophet (s) the position of the highest witness. God says, "*Thus We have made you a middle nation that you may be witnesses to the people, and that the Apostle may be a witness to you.*"[11]

God gave the same honor to his Prophet in another verse; "*They contemplated what they could not achieve, and they were vindictive only because God and His Apostle had enriched them out of His grace.*"[12] God says that He has enriched them, but also says that the Prophet (s) had a role in their enrichment. This is evidence of his great stature and that he is a means to God.

There are many other similar examples that show the great stature of the Prophet Muhammad (s). Each of the exam-

---

[9] Subḥani, *Al-'aqsam fi al-Qur'an al-Karim*, 52.

[10] The Holy Quran. Chapter 9 [The Repentance; Arabic: *Al-Tawba*]. Verse 94.

[11] The Holy Quran. Chapter 2 [The Cow; Arabic: *Al-Baqara*]. Verse 143.

[12] The Holy Quran. Chapter 9 [The Repentance; Arabic: *Al-Tawba*]. Verse 74.

ples needs to be detailed and explained. However, we can generally say that the verses indicate to us that true monotheism that God wishes us to follow is the monotheism that was practiced and taught by the Prophet (s). Whoever claims that they are monotheists but do not give the Prophet (s) the required respect and his due right, they have indeed been led astray. That is a deviance away from the path that God has ordained.

THE PROPHET AS A LEGISLATOR

Divine law is based on Divine Wisdom of what harms us and what helps us. God can also grant this knowledge to the Holy Prophet (s). Sometimes God legislates based on this knowledge directly and then commands the Prophet (s) to deliver the legislation. At other times, God commands the Prophet (s) to legislate according to that perfect knowledge God granted him and then deliver the legislation. Both ways of legislating are in line with God's will and God's Wisdom, and are thus free from error. But one is legislated directly by God while the other is legislated by God's command through the Prophet (s). In the first way, the Prophet (s) merely delivers the legislation, while in the second way the Prophet (s) is tasked with legislating as well as delivering the legislation.[13]

One of the unique responsibilities that God has given to the Holy Prophet (s) is this responsibility to legislate. The Muslims are in agreement that Islamic legislation is derived from the Quran and the traditions of the Prophet (s); as God has

---

[13] Al-Ḥaydari, *Buḥuth ḥawl al-Imamah*, 306.

said: *"Take whatever the Apostle gives you, and refrain from whatever he forbids you, and be wary of God."*[14]

That is because *"Nor does he speak out of [his own] desire: He is but revelation."*[15]

The Prophet (s) as a messenger of God did not only communicate God's direct legislation to us. Rather, the Prophet (s) was delegated the role of legislating according to God's knowledge, alongside his role as a messenger. This is clearly indicated in a number of narrations, including the following narration of Imam Sajjad (a):

> *[Imam Sajjad (a) was asked:] 'when were prayers made obligatory on the Muslims in the same fashion as they are right now?' The Imam (a) replied:* 'In Medina, when the message was revealed, Islam grew strong, and God made Jihad obligatory, the Messenger of God (s) added seven Raka'at; two to the noon prayers, two to the afternoon prayers, one in the dusk prayer, and two to the evening prayers. He kept the dawn prayer as it was made obligatory in Mecca, so as to hasten the ascension of the angels of the night to the heavens, and hasten the descent of the angels of the day to the Earth. Both the angels of the night and the angels of the day would be present with the Messenger of God (s) for the dawn prayers; that is why God says "Indeed the dawn recital is attended"[16] as it is attended by the Muslims as

---

[14] The Holy Quran. Chapter 59 [Arabic: *Al-Hashr*]. Verse 7.
[15] The Holy Quran. Chapter 53 [The Star; Arabic: *Al-Najm*]. Verses 3, 4.
[16] The Holy Quran. Chapter 17 [The Ascension; Arabic: *Al-Israa*]. Verse 78.

well as the angels of the night and the angels of the day. [17]

The Messenger (s) had the responsibility to legislate by God's permission. God deemed that His legislation through the Prophet (s) must be followed just as God Almighty's direct legislation must be followed. Any legislation decreed by the Prophet (s) is therefore binding on all Muslims.

THE PROPHET AS THE GREATEST MEANS TO GOD

The Meaning of the 'Means'

What does it mean that the Prophet (s) is the means to God?

God has created this world and has made everything in it contingent on the laws of cause and effect. Every phenomenon in this world has a cause that, by the will of God, produces an effect. For example, God has made water a cause of life in this world; He says: "*He who made the earth a place of repose for you, and the sky a canopy, and He sends down water from the sky and with it brings forth crops for your sustenance. So do not set up equals to God, while you know.*"[18] God characterizes these causes as His soldiers; "*No one knows the [soldiers] of your Lord except Him, and it is just an admonition for all humans.*"[19]

This connection between cause and effect does not in any way refute God's omnipotence. Natural causes do not have independent power. God's will is at all times sustaining this universe. Everything is subject to His will. The need for a

---

[17] Al-Amili, *Wasael Al-Shia*, 3:36.

[18] The Holy Quran. Chapter 2 [The Cow; Arabic: *Al-Baqara*], Verse 22.

[19] The Holy Quran. Chapter 74 [Arabic: *Al-Muddather*], Verse 31.

cause is a rational one, not limited to physical beings. So just as this physical world is bound by the laws of cause and effect that God has set, so too is the metaphysical world bound by the laws of cause and effect. God is the Guide and His guidance comes to us through angels and messengers. The Quran and the Prophet (s) are means through which God guides us.

Seeking closeness to God also requires utilizing the system of cause and effect. God has commanded us to seek these means to Him by following the guidance of the Quran and the Holy Prophet (s). These are the means to gain closeness to God. And when we examine the Quran and the traditions closely, we find that there are two ways to benefit from such means:

Firstly, there are the acts of worship that we have been guided to. The Commander of the Faithful (a) says:

> *The best means by which seekers of nearness to God, the Glorified, the Exalted, seek nearness, are: the belief in Him and His Prophet; fighting in His cause, for it is the high pinnacle of Islam; [belief] in the expression of devotion [to God], for it is the innate nature [of mankind]; the establishment of prayer, for it is [the basis of] religion; payment of zakat, for it is a compulsory obligation; fasting for the month of Ramadan, for it is the shield against chastisement; the performance of hajj of the House of God (i.e. Ka`bah) and its `umrah (i.e. pilgrimage outside the annual season) for these two acts banish poverty and wash away sins; regard for kinship, for it increases wealth and length of life; to give alms secretly, for it covers shortcomings; to give alms openly, for it protects against a bad death; and extend-*

ing benefits [to others] for it saves from positions of disgrace.[20]

Secondly, we can invoke the Prophet (s) – the greatest of God's creation and the closest to Him – as the means to God. In fact, this is the greatest and most important means to reach closeness to God, by following his guidance and seeking his intercession. The Commander of the Faithful (a) says in remembrance of the Prophet (s): *"My God, heighten his construction over the constructions of others, honor him when he comes to Thee, dignify his position before Thee, give him honorable position, and award him glory and distinction, and bring us out [on the Day of Judgment] among his party...."*[21]

Permissibility of Invoking the Prophet

Some schools of thought have asserted that invoking the Prophet (s) or seeking the aid of anyone but God is strictly impermissible. This misconception arose from confusion between invoking the Prophet (s) as a means to God, and ascribing a partner to Him – the Exalted. This notion is supported by a number of verses that say God alone can grant aid and warn against supplication to anyone but Him. God says:

Say, 'Invoke those whom you claim [to be gods] besides Him. They have no power to remove your distress, nor to bring about any change [in your state]. They [i.e. these creatures that have been taken as gods] are the ones who supplicate, seeking a [means] to their Lord, whoever is nearer [to

---

[20] Al-Radi, *Nahjul Balagha*, 1:215, Sermon 110.
[21] Ibid. Sermon 106.

Him], expecting His mercy and fearing His punishment.'
Indeed your Lord's punishment is a thing to beware of. [22]

When we go back to the exegesis of these verses, we find
that they were revealed as a rebuke to those who were taking the angels and the jinn as gods. The verses negate the
deification of these creatures and instills in the reader that
the only god worthy of worship is He who repels evil and
sustains life. All the other false deities that were taken up by
the pagans cannot supply mankind with these blessings.
Those creatures that have been worshipped instead of God,
they themselves worship God and receive their sustenance
from Him. Rather, the closest of these creatures seek the
means to God and His mercy. Therefore, these creatures
cannot be taken as deities.

After understanding the meaning of these verses, we see
that they do not support the proposed conclusion. We are
invoking the Prophet (s) as a means to God because He has
commanded us to *"seek the means of recourse to Him."*[23] No
Muslim regards the Prophet (s) as a deity. All the respect
and glorification that we pay to the Prophet (s) is due to the
fact that he is the closest servant to God. How can it be
claimed that we deify the Prophet (s) when all Muslims witness to the fact that he is a servant of God at least six times
a day? Any Muslim, during their daily prayers will repeat this
testimony of faith at least six times: *"I bear witness that there is
no god but God, alone without partner, and that Muhammad (s) is his
servant and Messenger."* When we invoke the Prophet (s) we
only seek him as an intercessor to God in answering our

---

[22] The Holy Quran. Chapter 17 [The Ascension; Arabic: *Al-Israa*]. Verse 56, 57.
[23] The Holy Quran. Chapter 5 [The Banquet; Arabic: *Al-Maeda*]. Verse 35.

calls. Or we ask God for the sake of the Prophet (s) and his proximity to Him to answer our calls. That's because we believe that without God's will, no creature – not even the Prophet (s) who is the greatest of God's creation – can bring sustenance or repel harm. This resolves the misconception that was proposed earlier. We repeat in our daily prayer our faith in God – "*You [alone] do we worship, and to You [alone] do we turn for help*"[24] – and that we turn to Him alone for help. This is not in contradiction to our belief in the Prophet (s) being the means to God because we believe that he cannot act independently of God. The rejected form of invocation is one that considers "that causes and mediums have a primary effect and independence in their action and impact, and it is improper to ascribe such a belief to any monotheist."[25]

Methods of Invoking the Prophet

Invocation of the Holy Prophet (s) as a means to God and seeking his intercession in fulfilling the individual's needs can take on many forms. We will list here a number of examples:

1. An individual can invoke the Prophet's (s) prayer by asking the Prophet (s) to pray for him.
2. An individual can invoke the Prophet's (s) person by asking God to answer his prayers for the sake of His Grand Prophet (s).
3. A person can ask the Prophet (s) for his intercession in this world or in the hereafter.

---

[24] The Holy Quran. Chapter 1 [The Opening; Arabic: *Al-Fatiha*]. Verse 5.
[25] Al-Subhani, *Fi Dhilal Al-Tawheed*, 644.

4. A person can ask the Prophet (s) directly for what-
    ever he needs. This form, in particular, raises mis-
    conceptions for some because they think that this is
    a form of ascribing partners to God. In reality, this
    form of invoking the Prophet (s) has nothing to do
    with ascribing partners to God, especially because of
    the great status that the Prophet (s) holds in his
    proximity to God. A person would only fall into the
    trap of ascribing a partner to God if they invoke the
    Prophet (s) believing that the Prophet (s) can act in-
    dependently of God's will and Lordship. And if no
    one actually believes this, as is generally the case,
    there is no problem in asking the Prophet (s) for his
    aid knowing the great status and abilities that God
    has bestowed on him. Rather, this form of invoking
    the Prophet (s) is a means for strengthening the in-
    dividual's faith because of the Prophet's (s) proximi-
    ty to God.

And there are other examples of invoking the Prophet (s),
many of them found in the actions of his companions and
the righteous servants of God who witnessed the time of
the Prophet (s). History is full of instances where individuals
of the highest faith and caliber have invoked the Grand
Prophet (s), and there are authors who have written books
about this subject.

We know that these methods of invoking the Prophet (s)
were allowed at the time of the Prophet (s), but are they also
permissible and effective after his passing? The answer to
this is simple: we believe that the Prophet (s) holds the same
sanctity in his death as he held in his lifetime. Therefore, we

must deal with him now as we would have dealt with him if he were alive. That is why many of the companions came to invoke the Prophet (s) at his grave and none of the other companions, including our immaculate Imam Ali (a), did anything to stop this. In other words, there was no ambiguity regarding the permissibility of this and the sanctity of the Prophet (s) even after departing this world.

The Importance of this Study

The issue of invoking the Prophet (s) is of great relevance to our daily lives. We will refer to a number of issues that make the subject so relevant:

1. This study is integral to understanding the Muslim faith and constitutes an important pillar of the individual's creed. Believing in the Prophet's (s) proximity to God and ability to intercede will lead to understanding the true monotheistic belief that has, at its core, the Prophet (s) as the path to God and the means to God's proximity in his person and teachings.

2. Believing in the ability and permissibility of invoking the Prophet (s) allows us to make full use of this great mercy that God has sent to all mankind.

3. The issue of invocation plays a big role in each individual's interaction with the Prophet (s) and knowing that he plays a role in our everyday lives. Rather, believing that he is the means to God will reinforce our interactions with him, as we will begin to understand that he continues to see the actions of all creation.

4. Invoking the Prophet (s) represents compliance with a divine command. God commanded us to seek the means to Him, and the Prophet (s) is the greatest means to God. Not seeking the means to God is a form of disobedience to God.

VISITATION OF THE PROPHET

In the Name of God, the most Beneficent, the most Merciful

Complete the hajj and the 'umrah for God's sake....[1]

God has commanded to complete the pilgrimage for His sake in all its facets and conditions.

In many verses, we are given specific commands and teachings regarding our life on this Earth. Alongside the verses of the Holy Quran, we take the words and actions of the Prophet (s) and His Household (a) as the primary sources of religious teachings. The Prophet (s) himself instructed us to do so when he said *"I leave amongst you two weighty things. If you were to hold fast to the both of them, you will never go astray after [my passing]. They are the Book of God and my progeny, my household."*[2] Holding fast to the Holy household (a) is equal to holding on to the Holy Quran because they will never be separated. And the authority of the Prophet (s) does not differ from the authority of the Quran because God equated the two in

---

[1] The Holy Quran. Chapter 2 [The Cow; Arabic: *Al-Baqara*]. Verse 196.

[2] Al-Saffar, *Basa'er Al-Darajat*, 433.

the verse: *"Take whatever the Apostle gives you, and refrain from whatever he forbids you."*[3]

At times, we find that the traditions of the Prophet (s) and the Holy Household (a) give us explanations of the Qur'anic verse that differ from the our understanding of the apparent meaning. That's because the Holy Quran has an apparent meaning, but also a deeper meaning such that, as some of our scholars have proposed, the verse can have multiple layers of meanings. Many verses contain a specific rule, but have other layers of meanings that are explained to us by our Prophet (s) and Immaculate Imams (a).

The verse above is one such verse; though its apparent meaning conveys a command from God to perform the pilgrimage – *Hajj* – to its full extent and in all of its parts, our Imams (a) also tell us that there is a deeper meaning to the verse. It's reported that Imam Ali (a) said,

> *Complete your* Hajj *by [seeking] the Prophet (s) if you travel to the House of God, as leaving him is distancing [yourself away from him] and you were commanded to [seek him]. [Complete your Hajj] by [seeking] the graves that God obliged you to fulfill their rights and visit. Ask for sustenance in their [i.e. the graves'] presence.*[4]

Completeness here is used to indicate perfection; meaning that *Hajj* is not perfected if it did not comprise of a number of additional act. The rewards of this perfected *Hajj* would not be attained without these additional acts. The *Hajj* that is performed without visitation of the Holy Prophet (s) is in

---

[3] The Holy Quran. Chapter 59 [Arabic: *Al-Hashr*]. Verse 7.

[4] Al-Sadouq, *Al-Khisal*, 2:616.

reality complete since the individual performed all the oblig-atory acts that comprise the core of the *Hajj*. However, it will only be perfected by visitation of the Prophet (s).

THE INDICATIONS OF VISITING THE PROPHET

Each act that is performed by any individual has its implica-tions and indications. When we visit the Holy Prophet (s) as his Holy Household (a) have commanded us, and when we visit the graves of the Immaculate Imams (a) that are buried in Medina, we give way to two great indications by these acts.

The first indication that this act carries is a belief in the sta-tus of the Prophet (s). Through this act, we manifest our be-lief in the core principles of our creed. We know that the core of Islamic teachings are embodied in the following creed: first is our belief in God's oneness – monotheism – and our belief in His absolute justice; second is our belief in the prophethood of our Holy Prophet Muhammad (s) and all other prophets, accompanied by our belief in the divine leadership of the Immaculate Imams (a); and third is the be-lief in the hereafter and the Day of Judgment. Through vis-itation of the Holy Prophet (s), we are making the following proclamations:

1. Our belief in God's oneness, as we are practically applying this belief by obeying His commands.
2. Our belief in the hereafter, as one of the purposes of *Hajj* is to bring closer the image of resurrection. It does that by placing everyone in those crowds at an equal footing, regardless of whether they are black or white, male or female, Arab or non-Arab,

young or old. Each station of the *Hajj* mirrors a station in the hereafter.

3. Our belief in prophethood as we proclaim our belief in the Prophet (s) and his Holy Progeny (a) by visiting them.

Through this we see that the true creed of an individual is manifested through this act.

The second indication is that of our eternal love for the Prophet (s) and his Holy Household (a). Islam teaches us the need to balance the intellectual and the emotional aspects of our life. We cannot rely solely on the intellect, as that will make us hardened and unspiritual, leading us to deviation. We cannot rely solely on emotion as well, as our emotions will outweigh our reason and also lead us to deviation. Instead we must be balanced in our approach. This is why Islam emphasizes the emotional connection with God and his vicegerents alongside the intellectual belief that we hold. Paying allegiance to the Prophet (s) and loving him is something that Islam calls for and is a show of true faith. It's also narrated that the Prophet (s) said,

> *None of you have reached the state of true belief until I become more beloved to you than yourselves, my household becomes more beloved to you than your household, my family becomes more beloved to you than your household, and my progeny becomes more beloved to you than your progeny.*[5]

---

[5] Al-Hindi, *Kanz Al-A'mal*, 1:41.

It's also narrated that the Prophet (s) said, "*Love God for what he sustains you with of His blessings. Love me for the love of God, the Exalted and Majestic. Love my Household (a) for your love of me.*"[6]

This emphasis on love and allegiance is not based on a haphazard whim. Rather, we were commanded to seek balance in our belief in God and His Prophet (s) so that faith can take its rightful and permanent place within ourselves. Visitation of the Prophet carries the manifestation of our love and allegiance to him. This love and allegiance is a cause for accepting his commands and refraining from what he has prohibited. The same thing is true for visiting the graves of the Holy Household.

THE REWARDS OF VISITING THE PROPHET

Invoking the Holy Prophet

One of the great blessings that God has given to the followers of the Holy Prophet (s) is making invocation of the Prophet (s) one of the causes of accepting the servants' supplications and answering of their prayers. The Prophet (s) has such a great status and proximity to God, that we believe that God will not turn back a servant that sought the Prophet (s) as a means to Him. God had accepted the repentance of Adam (a) through the name of Prophet Muhammad (a). And all sects of Islam believe this. The Prophet (s) said,

> *When Adam (a) committed the mistake [of choosing a harder option on himself, albeit an acceptable one], he said, 'Oh Lord, I ask You by Muhammad (s) that You forgive*

---

[6] Al-Majlisi, *Bihar Al-Anwar*, 67:14.

me.' God said, 'Oh Adam, how did you know Muhammad
and I have not yet created him?' Adam said, 'Oh Lord, be-
cause when You created me with your hand and breathed
in me of Your soul, I lifted my head and I saw on the pil-
lars of the throne it was written "there is no god but God
and Muhammad (s) is His messenger." So I knew that
You did not add to Your name anyone but the most beloved
creation to You.' So God the Exalted said: 'you are right,
oh Adam. He is the most beloved creation to Me. Because
you have asked me by his [status], I have forgiven you. If it
wasn't for Muhammad, I would have created you.'[7]

We are all dependent beings, weak in our existence. We seek
sustenance and strength from God. We are given the opportunity to ask God to grant us our needs and invoke the
greatest of His creations at the holy land where he is buried.
That is why we find that one of the etiquettes of visiting the
Prophet (s) is to fast three days asking in them all your
needs – this is, by the way, an exception from the obligation
to break the fast during travel.

Seeking Forgiveness

One of the best means of forgiveness is to seek refuge by
the grave of the Prophet (s). The Prophet (s) was given this
status as intercessor in his lifetime by the words of the holy
Quran – God says,

We did not send any apostle but to be obeyed by God's
leave. Had they, when they wronged themselves, come to you
[oh Muhammad] and pleaded to God for forgiveness, and

---

[7] Al-Samhudi, *Wafaa' Al-Wafa bi Akhbar Daar Al-Mustafa*, 2:419. Citing, Al-Nisabouri, *Al-Mustadrak*, 2:615.

the Apostle had pleaded for them [to God] for forgiveness, they would have surely found God All-Clement, All-Merciful.[8]

So having the Prophet (s) ask for God's forgiveness on behalf of a believer who has repented will surely lead to God's forgiveness.

This special quality was not taken away at the Prophet's (s) death, as we believe that he continues to hold the same status and capabilities after his death as he had during his lifetime. We believe that he hears our speech and answers our calls. He has an effect on this world after his death just as he had an effect on it during his life. His character is one and unchanged. He is not a passing memory. He did not turn into a corpse that cannot do harm or bring any benefit. Rather, he is a source of blessings by the will of God because he is given the status of intercessor by God and the ability to grant the needs and forgive the sins of the believers.

Al-O'tbi narrated the following story:

I was sitting at the grave of the Prophet (s) when a Bedouin walked in and said, 'Peace be upon you oh Messenger of God. I have heard God saying that He has revealed to you a truthful book in which He says "Had they, when they wronged themselves, come to you [oh Muhammad] and pleaded to God for forgiveness, and the Apostle had pleaded for them [to God] for forgiveness, they would have surely found God All-*

---

[8] The Holy Quran. Chapter 4 [The Women; Arabic: *Al-Nisaa*]. Verse 64.

113

Clement, All-Merciful.'[9] *So I have come to you seeking forgiveness for my sins, seeking you as an intercessor to my Lord.' He then recited a few verses of poetry, then he asked for forgiveness and left. My eyes overtook me [with sleep]. I saw the Prophet (s) in my dream and he said to me,* 'Oh O'tbi! Follow the Bedouin and give him glad tidings. God has forgiven him.' *So I left to follow him but did not find him.*[10]

Greeting of the Prophet

The traditions of the Holy Household (a) have told us that the Prophet (s) hears our greetings when we greet him and pray for him. Some may erroneously think that this does not hold any value. Rather, it is one of the greatest blessings we have been given. It will suffice to mention the following narration that Imam Ridha (a) narrates about Imam Hussein (a) – he said,

> *Imam Hussein (a) was present during a holiday in Medina. He went towards the Prophet (s). [Imam Hussein (a)] greeted [his grandfather] and then said to whoever was present, 'verily, today we have been favored over the people of all lands, whether Mecca or any other, because [of the fact that we] greeted the Messenger of God (s)*[11]

It suffices us to know the great value of greeting the Prophet (s) through this tradition. How great is such a greeting if Imam Hussein (a) regarded it as a virtue for the people of Medina that cannot be attained by any other city? There

---

[9] Ibid.

[10] Dah'lan, *Al-Durrar Al-Saniyya*, 21.

[11] Ibn Qawlaweih, *Kaamil Al-Ziyarat*, 547.

must, then, be some significant difference between greeting the Prophet (s) from a far distance, as opposed to greeting him at his grave.

A Guarantee of Intercession

The Prophet Muhammad (s) holds a great status and great proximity to God, such that God gave him the ability to intercede. There is no one in this world that does not need the intercession of the Prophet (s). It is narrated the following conversation was had in the presence of Imam Sadiq (a):

> *Imam Sadiq was asked about whether a believer has an ability to intercede [on the Day of Judgment]. Imam Sadiq said 'yes.' One of those present asked, 'will a believer need the intercession of Muhammad (s) on that day? Imam Sadiq (a) said 'yes.* A believer commits mistakes and sins, and there is no one that is not in need of the intercession of Muhamad on that day.' *Another asked him about the saying of the Prophet (s)* 'I am the master of the sons of Adam, and [I do not say this out of] pride.' *Imam Sadiq (a) said 'yes.* He will take the ring of the gate of paradise and open it. He will fall in prostration and God will say "raise your head. Intercede and you will be granted your intercession. Ask and you will be given." He will raise his head then fall again in prostration. God will say "raise your head. Intercede and you will be granted your intercession. Ask and you will be given." He will then raise his head. He will intercede and his

intercession will be granted. He will ask and he will be given.'*12*

The Prophet (s) has a great status – He was the one addressed in the verse "*It may be that your Lord will raise you to a praiseworthy station.*"[13] This verse has been interpreted to indicate the status of the Prophet (s) as intercessor.

It is narrated that Imam Sadiq said,

> *The Messenger of God (s) said 'whoever comes to Mecca in pilgrimage and does not visit me in Medina, I will turn away from him on the Day of Judgment. Whoever comes to visit me, he has earned my intercession. Whoever earns my intercession has earned paradise.*'[14]

Seeking Sustenance

One of the places at which it is highly recommended to ask for sustenance and blessings is at the grave of the Prophet (s) and the graves of the holy Household (a). This is yet another indication of the Prophet's (s) great merits.

---

[12] Al-Tabatabaei, *Al-Mizan*, 2:176.
[13] The Holy Quran. Chapter 17 [The Ascension; Arabic: *Al-Israa*]. Verse 79.
[14] Al-Kulayni, *Al-Kafi*, 4:548.

THE GUARDIANSHIP OF AHLULBAYT

In the Name of God, the most Beneficent, the most Merciful

Your guardian is only God, His Apostle, and the faithful who maintain the prayer and give the zakat while bowing down. [1]

The joyous occasions that we celebrate in relation to Ahlulbayt (a) contain amazing proof regarding their status. Take the example of Imam Ali (a) when he was bowing down in his prayer; the Imam (a) gave his ring to a poor man that was asking for assistance while he was in that state. With this unprecedented deed, God affirmed the lofty status of Ali (a) by His Holy words: *"Your guardian is only God, His Apostle, and the faithful who maintain the prayer and give the zakat while bowing down."* [2] Divine guardianship was bestowed upon he who performed this magnanimous deed – that was the Commander of the Faithful Ali (a). This was performed in the month of Dhil Hijja of the Islamic calendar.

---

[1] The Holy Quran. Chapter 5 [The Banquet; Arabic: *Al-Maeda*]. Verse 55.
[2] Ibid.

Another important event took place on the 24th of Dhil Hi-jja, that is what became known as the Day of Mubahala. On that day the entirety of faith was embodied in the Messenger of God, Ali, Fatima, Al-Hassan, and Al-Hussain (peace and blessings be upon them all) to stand against disbelief and the denial of faith. This day manifested not only honor for the Commander of the Faitful (a) and Ahlulbayt (a) but meanings within the religion and its guardianship. God describes this honor and meaning in the following verse:

> *Should anyone argue with you concerning him, after the knowledge that has come to you, say, 'Come! Let us call our sons and your sons, our women and your women, our souls and your souls, then let us pray earnestly, and call down God's curse upon the liars.*[3]

Last but not least, let us not forget the three days that Imam Ali (a) and his family fasted in honor of a vow they made before God for the health of their children. They stayed without eating food for three consecutive nights, because on those nights needy people knocked on their doors and they gave all that they had to help them – which was only the food they had to break their fast. Because of these noble acts God revealed an entire chapter in the Holy Quran in the honor of Ali (a) and his family, to be recited by every Muslim until the Day of Judgment. This is one of the many gifts God gave them – this family that gave everything they had for the sake of God. They knew everything is for God, so they thanked Him by giving it all to Him in such an amazing show of virtue.

---

[3] The Holy Quran. Chapter 3 [Arabic: *Aal Imran*]. Verse 61

These events are indicative of the status and honor of Ahlulbayt (a) with the Holy Prophet (s) and ultimately with God. To examine all of these events and their meanings would require an intricate study with sophisticated depth. For the individuals of study here are the guardians of faith, the Household of the Prophet (s) – Ali, Fatima, Hassan, and Hussain (peace be upon them). But the question will arise, why is there an emphasis on Ali (a) and his family, rather than other Muslims or companions of the Prophet's (s) time? Our religion was not established on the basis of nepotism or the rise of dynasties. Thus, there is no doubt that the distinction of Ali (a) and his family would be based on objective reasons and features that made them exceptional and unique. Of the many components that make Ahlulbayt (a) exceptionally excellent, we will discuss three primary ones:

1. Guardianship and the Connection with God and Creation
2. The Authority and Purity of Ahlulbayt (a)
3. The Qualifications for Guardianship

GUARDIANSHIP AND THE CONNECTION WITH GOD

The greatness of Ahlulbayt (a) cannot be simplified in any one aspect. Their worship of God was so sublime no other member of humanity could compare. Their knowledge was so supreme that it surpassed everyone else's. They inherited the knowledge, wisdom and character of the Holy Prophet (s). They are the closest people to God, for God purified them a perfect purification. Moreover, when the Holy Quran establishes their guardianship and discusses their status it points to something extremely important. Divine guardianship and this lofty status with God comes only through one giving himself completely to God through worship and generosity. This was reflected in Imam Ali's (a) care for the creation around him. Ali (a) deserved to be in the position of guardianship because he upheld prayers, paid alms, and gave charity in the state of prayer – an unprecedented display of generosity. Ahlulbayt (a) fulfilled their vow to God by not only fasting three days but by feeding the poor, the orphan, and the captive their own portions of food. All of that was done in worship of God.

> *They fulfill their vows and fear a day whose ill will be widespread. For the love of Him, they feed the needy, the orphan and the prisoner, [saying,] 'We feed you only for the sake of God. We desire no reward from you, nor thanks. Indeed we fear a frowning and fateful day from our Lord.' So God saved them from that day's ills and graced them with freshness [on this faces] and joy [in their hearts].[4]*

The status of Ahlulbayt (a) came by way of being completely dissolved in worship and submission to God. The highest levels of connection to God occur when a person disconnects from everything and holds on only to God. It's almost as if he doesn't even feel any of the physical beings in his midst, and only senses the encompassing presence of God. Nonetheless, what is even higher in status of worship is that you are not distracted by one worship from another. When Imam Ali (a) gave away his ring in charity, he was not distracted from his remembrance of God in prayer. Rather, he was so dissolved in the worship of God he worshipped him

---

[4] The Holy Quran. Chapter 76 [Man; Arabic: *Al-Insan*]. Verses 7-11.

even further with the additional act of charity. This is the individual that was deserving of being a divine guardian. He worshipped God so truly that he did not forget about caring for the people in his midst. He took care of people even as he prayed. This is simpler said than done. That act alone, amongst all the magnanimous acts of Ali (a), could not have been done by anyone else in the same way. Practically speaking, another person would have been distracted from his prayer and paid attention to the poor man who asked for charity. Or a person in the same situation would have been distracted by their prayer and not have paid attention to the one who sought help. But to combine both of these forms of worship, in one individual, in one moment... that can only be accomplished by Ali (a) and the likes of Ali (a).

THE AUTHORITY AND PURITY OF AHLULBAYT (A)

God willed for Ahlulbayt (a) to be purified, for He said: "*Indeed God desires to repel all impurity from you, O People of the Household, and purify you with a thorough purification.*"[5]

This verse encompasses a number of significant topics like the following: why did God's will focus on the Household of the Holy Prophet (s)? Who are the members of the Household that God has purified? Is this will one that is legislative or creational? Is this purification one that suggests they were impure or that they are purified in their very essence?

What concerns us in our study here is the issue of purification and its meaning. Before delving into that we should pay

---

[5] The Holy Quran. Chapter 33 [The Factions; Arabic: *Al-Ahzab*]. Verse 33.

attention to a significant point: when we look at our reli-gious laws we find a number of issues that deal with differ-ent types of authority or guardianship. For example, a child is not allowed to spend his money or any other money without the permission of his guardian. The guardian in this situation could be his father, his grandfather, or whoever else as detailed in Islamic law. Another example is that of marriage; specifically, a young lady generally cannot marry except by the permission of her guardian. Another example of authority is that reserved for jurists – the Guardianship of the Jurist (*Wilayat-al-Faqih*) – that can vary in the breadth of its jurisdiction depending on the jurist's theory on the matter. Guardianship can be in different shapes and forms, but what these forms share in common is that they all have limits and restrictions. Take the example of the guardian who has the authority of what and how his child spends their money. In order for the guardian's authority to be val-id, the guardian must be mentally healthy and having the best interests of his child in mind. Likewise, a father's au-thority over his daughter's marriage is also contingent on several factors. For instance, if the girl's father does not grant permission for marriage when both parties are mature and suitable for one another according to religious and common sense standards, the father's permission is no longer required for that marriage to be valid. In addition, the jurist must also have the prerequisites of justice, scholar-ship, intellect, etc. in order to legitimately practice his au-thority as a jurist. Each one of these forms of guardianship is limited by prerequisites and a scope of authority. The scope of guardianship of Ahlulbayt (a), however, is not re-stricted in the sense that these other forms are restricted.

Their authority comes second only to that of God and His Prophet (s). It is similar to how the Prophet's (s) authority cannot be restricted, as he has more authority over the believers than they do over themselves. This authority is ordained by God as mentioned in the verse we opened this chapter with. This same authority is given to the Imam (a), unrestricted and second only to that of the Holy Prophet (s).

There is a special characteristic of those that hold this guardianship – infallibility. The other forms of guardianship have restrictions because the holders of those positions are subject to error. The guardianship of the Imam (a), however, is unrestricted because the Imam (a) is infallible and will not fall into error or sin. Thus, he will not abuse the authority he holds because he is immaculate and untainted by any form of impurity. This is where the verse on purification comes in, affirming this blessed fact and manifesting God's will. Note that the verse included the word "only" (in Arabic *innama*) for emphasis and reassurance that it is Ahlulbayt (a) who are pure from any form of sully. Consider the following:

First, this purification is from all impurities given the original Arabic use of "*Al*" which gives the application of a broad and encompassing scope to all that is considered "*rijs*" (impurity), be it material or moral. This also applies to every sense of sin or transgression and any level of defect in action or character. They are free from all such impurity.

Second, the Ahlulbayt (a) are purified in every single way. Impurity is prohibited from them before the age of maturity and after, in delivering the laws of God and otherwise. To do anything impure, be it with intent, or out of forgetfulness or ignorance, does not happen with Ahlulbayt – because God has guaranteed their purity. Regardless if a person were to fall into some form impurity, knowingly or not knowingly, they have fallen into it. The difference may be that one deserves punishment while the other doesn't; however, the ignorance of the impurity does not change the state of the impurity itself. Thus, such a person would not be pure in every sense; ignorance and forgetfulness do not work with the infallibility and purity of Ahlulbayt (a).

Third, this purity from God translates into an extremely high level of piety, whereby they do not commit any sins nor do they make mistakes – with God's help and protection. This does not mean that he *cannot* commit wrong, because purification does not nullify free will. Rather, the Imam (a) *chooses not* to commit wrong because he clearly sees the heinous immorality in opposing God. The Imam's (a) infallibility is based on knowledge. Take the example of a person who sees a glass of water filled with a clearly poisonous liquid. He knows it's filled with poison and thus will not drink from the glass. He has every capability to actually drink from the glass but he chooses not to. This is how the Imam (a) looks at sin – he can commit it but chooses not to. If the Imam's (a) infallibility was forced against his will he would not be the human example and role model for people, who are to avoid sin out of their own volition. The Prophets and Imams are humans with free will. They face many of the challenges we face. But because of their qualifications, God's wisdom blessed them with special knowledge, practically guaranteeing their infallibility. Thus, they are the standard for everyone else to be measured up against.

Finally, this purity has been specially designated for God's prophets and vicegerents for the weight of the responsibility that has been heaped over their shoulders. This infallibility is of benefit to all people, because when the vicegerent is infallible his wisdom and grace affects everyone else.

THE QUALIFICATIONS FOR GUARDIANSHIP

Unrestricted guardianship can only be given to those with the requisite aptitude of knowledge, awareness, and ability to hold such divine responsibility. All other forms of guardianship must be granted through the one with unrestricted guardianship, and according to the conditions set forth by the one with that unrestricted guardianship. The Holy Quran points to this qualitative requirement embodied in the virtues of patience and certainty: "*When they had been patient and had conviction in Our signs, We appointed amongst them imams to guide [the people] by Our command.*"[6]

Being an Imam, which is the title of the vicegerent, is realized through two primary virtues mentioned above in the verse: patience and certainty.

Patience

Patience is by far one of the most essential traits of imamate. A person who is chosen by God as a leader and guide for humanity should without a doubt have patience. God refers to leaders with patience in the following verse: "*So be*

---

[6] The Holy Quran. Chapter 32 [Arabic: *Al-Sajda*]. Verse 24.

patient just as the resolute among the apostles were patient…"[7] One of the traits of the Messengers of Great Resolve is patience. God describes his vicegerents, who He holds in high regard, as the patient ones. In fact, one of the reasons for their lofty position with God is patience. Even regarding other Prophets, such as Prophet Job (a) (*Ayyūb*), God said: "*…Indeed, We found him to be patient. What an excellent servant! Indeed he was a penitent [soul]."*[8]

If we look back at the Commander of the Faithful (a) and the rest of Ahlulbayt (a), we would be speechless – unable to describe the tribulations they endured, which they faced with more than just patience. They persevered with contentment and complete submission to the will of God. Imam Ali (a) did not live a day in his life where he did not face a trial, tribulation or tragedy until he departed from this world. What greater tragedy could there be than having your rights taken away and your wife harmed and abused in such a way? In this regard he would say, "*So I adopted patience although there was pricking in the eye and suffocation (of mortification) in the throat…"*[9] This family – the Household of Muhammad (s) – endured more pain and suffering than any other family could. What tragedy could be compared to that of Al-Hussain (a)? What calamity measures up to that of the Prophet's (s) daughter Fatima (a)? And what oppression was seen like the oppression endured by Al-Hassan (a)? Despite all this, these saints met the trials and pain with patience. Thus, God honored them with guardianship over mankind.

[7] The Holy Quran. Chapter 46 [The Dunes; Arabic: *Al-Ahqaf*]. Verse 35.
[8] The Holy Quran. Chapter 38 [Arabic: *Sad*]. Verse 44.
[9] Al-Radi, *Nahjul Balagha*, 1:31, Sermon 3.

Certainty

Knowledge that is not penetrated by doubt, certainty, is essential in the scheme of guardianship and imamate. The Holy Quran discusses this type of knowledge or certainty which is a result of witnessing the divine realm. This realm mandates certainty that doesn't rely on induction and evidence, rather it comes as a result of witnessing the divine realities. *"Thus did We show Abraham the dominions of the heavens and the earth, that he might be of those who possess certitude."*[10]

The discussion on the meaning of divine realm and how witnessing it takes place is a deep and lengthy one. Nonetheless, note that presential (non-acquired) certainty is much more important than all of the levels of faith.

Imam Al-Sadiq (a) said, *"Faith is better than submission, certainty is better than faith, and there is nothing dearer than certainty."*[11] Such certainty is built on knowledge, but not just any normal knowledge that is acquired through the senses. Rather, it is presential knowledge that is not acquired through the physical senses. With this type of knowledge, the subject matter is present to the individual without the medium of a mental image. The person simply senses the presence and is aware of the presence. This is consciousness of something present to the person. Some of our scholars have offered the following as an example of presential knowledge, "knowing oneself, and one's abilities of movement and realization. We know of our own ability to think and imag-

---

[10] The Holy Quran. Chapter 6 [The Cattle; Arabic: *Al-Anaam*]. Verse 75.
[11] Al-Kulayni, *Al-Kafi*, 2:51.

ine,"[12] by presence, not needing mental images, not by that learning process.

Now what kind of knowledge did the Commander of the Faithful (a) encompass? When he was the one to say, "*O people! Ask me before you lose me, because certainly I am acquainted with the passages of the sky more than the passages of the earth…*"[13] What a challenge the Imam (a) posed, for only a man with knowledge granted by God could stand with such certainty.

In regards to Imam Ali's (a) certainty, we stand puzzled before his words: "*If the veils were removed, I would not increase in certainty.*" This man stood with the highest level of certainty, which the vicegerents of his spiritual lineage inherited from him. Because of their virtues and knowledge they were blessed with God's decree to make them the successors to the Prophet and Divinely appointed guardians to the people. This guardianship, as we learned, is essential in the scheme of faith and religion. As narrated on behalf of Imam Al-Baqir (a), "*Islam was built on five: prayer, charity, fasting, pilgrimage, and guardianship. And no call was made greater than that of guardianship. People took the first four and neglected the fifth – guardianship…*"[14]

Our narrations point to the significance of guardianship, specifically emphasizing the vitality of allegiance to the vicegerents of God. Consider the following tradition from Imam Al-Sadiq (a): "*Our guardianship (and allegiance to us) is the*

---

[12] Al-Yazdi, *Al-Manhaj Al-Jadeed fe Ta'leem Al-Falsafa*, 1:173.

[13] Al-Radi, *Nahjul Balagha*, 2:130, Sermon 189.

[14] Al-Kulayni, *Al-Kafi*, 2:15.

guardianship of God (and allegiance to God), which no prophet was sent without (paying such allegiance)."[15]

Imam Al-Hassan (a) said, *"Allegiance to Ali (a) is written in all the books of the prophets, for God did not send a prophet that did not pay allegiance to Muhammad (s) and Ali (a)..."*[16]

---

[15] Ibid, 1:362.

[16] Al-Saffar, *Basa'er Al-Darajat*, 92.

THE RIGHTS OF AHLULBAYT

In the Name of God, the most Beneficent, the most Merciful

We made them imams, guiding by Our command, and We revealed to them [concerning] the performance of good deeds, the maintenance of prayers, and the giving of zakat, and they used to worship Us.[1]

The Imams of Ahlulbayt (a) have a special position in the hearts of Muslims in general and in the hearts of their followers especially. They are the true caliphs and rightful successors of the Prophet (s) and the inheritors of his knowledge. He made them the lanterns of guidance and the flag bearers of truth. The traditions in this regards are too many to count; nonetheless, we will mention a few of the most important ones that evidence the lofty status that God has given them.

As narrated by Ahmad bin Hanbal, the Prophet (s) said:

I am leaving with you the two weighty things. If you hold on to them both you will never stray after me. One of them is greater than the other, the Book of God, and my Ahlulbayt

---

[1] The Holy Quran. Chapter 21 [The Prophets; Arabic: *Al-Anbiya*]. Verse 73.

(a). These two will not separate from each other until they return to me on the Day of Judgment.[2]

Rafi', the servant of Abathar (r), narrated:

I saw Abathar (r) hold onto the gate of the Ka'ba saying: 'Whoever knows me knows me as Jundub Al-Ghafari, and whoever does not know me then I am Abathar. I heard the Messenger of God (s) say: "My Ahlulbayt (a) to you is like the Ark of Noah. Whoever boards the ark is saved and whoever falls behind will drown..."'[3]

Regardless of the differences between the schools of thought on the application of these traditions to indicate general leadership or moral and religious guidance, all Muslims believe that Ahlulbayt (a) have rights upon the Muslims given their lofty status with God. It is enough to point at the following verse where God tells the Holy Prophet (s) to *"say, 'I do not ask you any reward for it except the love of [my] relatives.'"*[4]

The message of Islam saved humanity from the darkness and brought it into the light. That same message demanded that the Muslims fulfill their obligations toward the religion and the Holy Prophet (s), who has rights and favor over all Muslims. He is the one who brought forth this divine message and guided the people, and his reward is the love of his near of kin. Thus, those near of kin – the family of the Prophet (s) – have rights that God mandated up on us. Regardless of the perspective on who is included in this defini-

---

[2] Al-Majlisi, *Bihar Al-Anwar*, 23:106. Citing, Ibn Hanbal, *Musnad Ahmad*, 3:26.
[3] Ibid, 23:105.
[4] The Holy Quran. Chapter 42 [The Prophets; Arabic: *Al-Anbiya*]. Verse 23.

tion of 'household' and who this applies to, the Imams of Ahlulbayt (a) are without a doubt the clearest members of that household. From the perspective of the School of Thought of Ahlulbayt (the Shia), the Imams (a) are the class of persons intended to be identified under this label of near or kin. In the other schools of thought, the Imams (a) are at least the clearest application of the label. Thus, there is no disagreement between the Muslims regarding the existence of the rights of the twelve Imams (a).

The books of the Muslims, in all their differences in creed and outlooks, are full of praise of the Holy Household (a). Except for rare outliers, all Muslims realize the greatness of Ahlulbayt (a) and sing their praises.

KNOWING AHLULBAYT

The first primary right of Ahlulbayt (a) is the obligation upon us to learn about them and know them. How can one love the Prophet (s)'s near of kin without first knowing about them? Love follows knowledge. Furthermore, there are numerous texts that illustrate the obligation of every Muslim to know their Imam. The person who does not know their Imam is considered ignorant and astray. Some of the texts point to the obligation of knowing the Imam, and others go further to include the obligation to pay allegiance to him as well – which stems from the initial obligation of knowing the Imam. Mohammad bin Othman bin Saeed Al-Zayyat (r) narrates,

> I heard my father say: 'Imam Hassan Al-Askari (a) was asked about the words of his forefathers regarding the Earth not being without a proof of God upon His creation until

the Day of Judgment. And that whoever dies without know-
ing the Imam of his time will die the death of ignorance. The
Imam would respond: "this truth is as clear as day.*"[5]*

Another narration comes from Musnad Ahmad, "The Prophet (s) said: *'The person who dies without an Imam dies the death of ignorance.'"*[6]

Though Muslims have differed on the application and details of imamate, in reality they all agree on the obligation of its existence and one's acknowledgement of it. The essential element that there must be an Imam for the Muslims is mandatory and there is a consensus on that; thus, it goes without saying that one should strive to know, follow and be loyal to that Imam.

The School of Thought of Ahlulbayt (a) believes that the matter pertaining to imamate pertains directly to God. The general populous has no role in dictating who the Imam is, rather the Imam is chosen only by God as a representative and guardian of the faith. There are a few issues that are significant for us to discuss to clarify the importance of the Imam. Take note that if we fall short in our obligations toward the Imam, it does not affect the Imam's status at all. The Imam is God's vicegerent by the decree of God, regardless if people follow or oppose him. Just as the prophethood of the Prophet (s) is independent of the people's acceptance or rejection, so is the divinely appointed Imamate. Therefore, knowing the Prophet or the Imam is for the benefit of the people alone. Not knowing them is the people's loss.

---

[5] Al-Nouri, *Mustadrak Al-Wasail*, 18:187.

[6] Ibn Hanbal, *Musnad Ahmad*, 4:96.

Knowledge of Religion is Contingent Upon Knowing the Imam

The Imam has a unique and significant role in leading people towards God, because the Imam is the proof of God. God appoints the Imam as a testimony and witness upon all other creatures. The Imam lives up to God's standards for human excellence and goes through trials and tribulations, succeeding with flying colors. He is thus a role model by his very existence and a living testament practicing what God tells him to preach. Moreover, the Imam testifies on behalf of or against all others because God grants him a deep awareness of their actions. The Imam is the living medium and connection to God Almighty, delivering and protecting the message of the Prophet (pbuh) immaculately. Knowing the Imam is the way to knowing God. It is impossible for us to know the true knowledge of religion, which is the path toward knowing God, without going through the medium that God appointed as a testimony and proof for His religion. Imam Al-Sadiq (a) said, *"This Earth will always have a scholar that people need, yet he does not need the people, and he knows what is permissible and what is forbidden (of the laws of God)."*[7]

The Imam's role is not simply in knowing what is permissible and forbidden; rather he knows everything that is related to religion from its principles to its branches. The elements of religion and faith are not complete without knowing the Imam. Imam Al-Sadiq (a) said,

> *God refused for things to be without a cause, so he created a cause for every thing. For every cause he made an explanation, and for every explanation there is a science. For every*

---

[7] Al-Majlisi, *Bihar Al-Anwar*, 23:50.

science there is a [professing teacher]. Those who know him know him and those who are ignorant of him are ignorant of him. Regardless, they are the Messenger of God and us [his Holy Household].[8]

No matter how much knowledge a person attains, he will not be able to learn all the knowledge of religion without the Imam. One of the clearest examples of this is the clashing of Muslims of different schools of thought on a number of intellectual issues to which they have found no solid answers or solutions to. Many of these issues cannot be resolved except by connecting to the Master of the Message, which can't be made in our time due to the loss of Prophet (s). Only one who holds the heritage and knowledge of the Prophet (s) can resolve these problems. Thus, not knowing that person hinders our ability to find solutions to our problems.

The lack of direct access to the living Imam today is not because God did not create him and sustain him. Moreover, it is not because the Imam himself does not want to help us. But, rather, the actions of the oppressors and other issues associated with the human exercise of free will prevent the Imam from being directly accessible for now. The next best solution is for us to refer to the upright expert scholars who analyze the heritage of the Prophet (s) and the Imams (a) and try to come as close as possible to the truth, given the circumstances. The living Imam himself wants us to do this during these trying times in which we lack direct access to him. When the world is ready and when the living Imam's followers have prepared the grounds for his rise to the pub-

---

[8] Al-Kulayni, *Al-Kafi*, 1:183.

lic scene once again, with that we will be among those who regain direct access to him, God-willing.

Knowing the Imam is Protection from Sedition

The Holy Quran and the pure Tradition of the Prophet (s) are not enough on their own to protect the religion and ensure that it is not corrupted. Throughout history there were hundreds of groups that led people astray claiming to be within the fold of Islam by asserting their attachment to the Quran and Tradition. The Quran and the Tradition include some statements that are summations, others that are specific, some that are unambiguous and others that are ambiguous. Imam Ali (a) would describe these as having many levels of interpretation. Thus, not everyone will agree on all of the meanings, evidenced by the dozens of different interpretations and exegeses. If everything in the Quran and the Tradition was completely clear then the Muslims would not fall into disagreement.

There must be someone that people go back to in matters of disagreement. Without that subject of reference or return, it would only mean more division and disagreement between people. The person we should go back to must have certain characteristics to be qualified in order for people to return to in matters of disagreement. Otherwise, without such qualifications there would be division instead of unity amongst people in understanding the Quran and the Tradition. The ones God directly provides for us to return to must be infallible from mistake and forgetfulness, because if they were fallible they would not be able to properly safeguard the affairs of people form further disparity. The Commander of the Faithful (a) said, *"Obedience is to*

God, His Prophet, and the vicegerents. Obedience to the vicegerents has been ordained because they are infallible, pure, and do not order people to do wrong."[9]

Ahlulbayt (a) have emphasized the significance of knowing the Imam because he is the subject of reference and emulation in upholding and protecting the religion. The Imam prevents us from falling into sedition by bringing us back to him in matters of disagreement. Imam Al-Baqir (a) said, *"Hold people to three things: to know the Imams, to take what the Imams have given them, and to go back to them whenever they are in disagreement."*[10]

Being saved from sedition, disparity and being distanced from the wrong path is possible only through knowing the true Imams, accepting them, and returning to them in matters of disagreement. When the community falls into disparity, the way to rescue is the ship of salvation that the Prophet (s) advised his followers with – his Holy Household. Recall his words, *"I am leaving with you the two weighty things. If you hold on to them both you will never stray after me…"*[11]

In addition, knowing one's Imam will give a person the same result as being present at a time when God makes His religion supreme over the entire Earth. In such a time, justice and equality will fill the Earth. There will be no division, disunity, or disparity, for God's truth will be evident and clear. The message that God sent with all His prophets until the Seal of Prophets, Muhammad (s), will be manifested with the Awaited Mahdi (aj). This time will be without a

---

[9] Al-Sadouq, *'Ilel Al-Sharai'*, 1:123.

[10] Al-Kulayni, *Al-Kafi*, 1:390.

[11] Al-Majlisi, *Bihar Al-Anwar*, 23:106.

doubt unique in comparison to any other time in history. Thus, a believer who knows their Imam is rendered like the one who will live at the described age of justice and equality, because such a person is protected from sedition and deviation. Zurara narrates that, "Abu Abdillah (a) said, '*Know your Imam. By knowing him, the hastening or delay [of his reappearance] will not affect you.*'"[12]

Knowing the Imam Guarantees the Acceptance of Deeds

Two things affect our fate in the afterlife: our beliefs and our deeds. Together both these will indicate whether we will find ourselves in heaven or hell. The correct beliefs with no action or deeds risks an unwanted end. Likewise, having seemingly good deeds without sound creed and intent, does not hold enough solid ground to qualify for paradise. The Quran describes the disbelievers' deeds as null and void due to the fact that they do not stem from correct faith and are therefore built on improper intentions. Thus, the role of creed and intention is greater than that of other deeds but still each holds its weight and importance. Prayers for forgiveness and intercession can be made for a person who dies with the correct creed; however, not the same can be said for one who dies inexcusably rejecting the truth. On this basis, knowing the Imam is emphasized. For he is the one who guides us to the path of God. Knowing him allows us to be on the right track of actions and deeds for the sake of God. Without knowing the Imam we will die the death of ignorance, as told to us by the Prophet (s) himself. Our actions will spring out of our true faith and correct creed, knowing the Imam of our time who is our connection to

---

[12] Al-Kulayni, *Al-Kafi*, 1:371.

the message of the Prophet (s). Do note that simply acknowledging the existence of the Imam is not enough. Knowing the Imam means that we obey, bid loyalty, and love the Imam. That kind of relationship will guarantee the acceptance of our deeds by God's grace.

Abi Hamza came to Imam Al-Baqir (a) and said, "O' son of the Messenger of God, there is a man who fasts all day, prays all night, gives charity, and we do not know anything but good about him. But he does not recognize [your authority as the Imam]." To that the Imam (a) smiled and said, "*...If a man were to remain in prostration between the cornerstone [of the Ka'ba] and the shrine [of Abraham (a)] until his soul departs this world, and yet he does not recognize our authority, none of that will help him.*"[13] The Imam (a) also said, "*Whoever dies and in his heart is hatred towards us, Ahlulbayt, and paid allegiance to our enemies, God will not accept from him a single deed.*"[14] If someone has access to the truth and chooses to turn a blind eye, or sees the truth and chooses to cover it up, that person's seemingly good deeds cannot hide their true colors from God Almighty.

LOVING AHLULBAYT

When we talk about loving Ahlulbayt (a) we're not referring to simply emotion and sentiment. Our religion considers the emotional dimension of the human being to have a great and long-lasting effect in moving a person in any direction he chooses. Most deviations that we see in the world are caused by a defect in one's emotional course. Thus, Islam

---

[13] Al-Nouri, *Mustadrak Al-Wasail*, 1:150.
[14] Ibid.

has given much importance to filling this emotional aspect instead of leaving it vacant to be filled by other detrimental things. Rather, Islam would fill the hearts of the believers with love for God and his vicegerents, from one aspect, and fill it with innocence and opposition to the enemies of God and his vicegerents, from another aspect. The Holy Quran stressed on the importance of taking a position in regards to who we love and who we loathe:

> *Among the people are those who set up compeers besides God, loving them as if loving God—but the faithful have a more ardent love for God—though the wrongdoers will see, when they sight the punishment, that power, altogether, belongs to God, and that God is severe in punishment.*[15]

If someone were to inexcusably disrespect and wickedly challenge the one most beloved to us, how would we feel toward that person? Such a person's actions would make our hearts turn away. We would not show them approval for their wrongdoing at all. Islam emphasizes that expressing one's love for God should supersede all other expressions of love to any other being. One who believes in God should not express love to those who stand to arrogantly oppose and blatantly challenge God, the Beloved Lord. Thus, God states in the Holy Quran:

> *You will not find a people believing in God and the Last Day endearing those who oppose God and His Apostle even though they were their own parents, or children, or brothers, or kinsfolk. [For] such, He has written faith into their hearts and strengthened them with a spirit from Him. He*

---

[15] The Holy Quran. Chapter 2 [The Cow; Arabic: *Al-Baqara*]. Verse 165.

*will admit them into gardens with streams running in them,
to remain in them [forever], God is pleased with them, and
they are pleased with Him. They are God's confederates.
Look! The confederates of God are indeed felicitous!*[16]

If only those who have gone astray would come to their
senses and make amends… A true believer would reflect
God's attribute of mercy and hope that all people would
choose to receive God's mercy and love. But God is also
Wise and there are those who choose to turn away from
God's love and challenge God. It would not be wise to treat
such evil-doers with the same mercy and love as that of a
faithful believer. A true believer, thus, would not love those
in such a wretched state. Because of their own choices, such
evil-doers deserve to be distanced from God's special love
and mercy.

We cannot claim to be believers in God if our hearts are not
filled with love for God and his vicegerents, especially His
Honorable Messenger (s) and his Holy Household (a). It is
enough that God has made the reward of the message to be
their love:

*Such is the good news that God gives to His servants who
have faith and do righteous deeds! Say, 'I do not ask you
any reward for it except the love of [my] relatives.' Whoever
performs a good deed, We shall enhance its goodness for
him. Indeed God is all-forgiving, all-appreciative.*[17]

Dozens of narrations have underlined the significance of
love for the Prophet (s) and the Imams (a), with some con-

---

16 The Holy Quran. Chapter 58 [Arabic: *Al-Mujadala*]. Verse 22.
17 The Holy Quran. Chapter 42 [The Prophets; Arabic: *Al-Anbiya*]. Verse 23.

142

sidering that such love is the foundation of faith and religion. This emphasis goes back to having people live with their entire existence for God and His vicegerents. The emotional dimension of our being can be more effective than even the clearest logical proofs that the mind sees. Thus, after understanding these truths, Islam stresses filling our hearts with the love of God, His Prophet (s), and Ahlulbayt (a) instead of being blinded by other love that has no basis at all.

The Holy Prophet (s) said, *"Islam is bare. Its clothing is bashfulness and its ornament is dignity. Its zeal is righteous action and its mainstay is devotion. Everything has a foundation and the foundation of Islam is the love for us, Ahlulbayt."*[18] The Prophet (s) also said, *"Love for me and my family is beneficial in seven great situations: at death, in the grave, during resurrection, when the deeds are written, during judgment, when deeds are being weighed, and [in walking along] the path..."*[19]

FOLLOWING AHLULBAYT

Our faith is not complete simply by knowing who our Imams are and professing love for them. Rather, the foundation upon which our faith is based on is completed only through loyalty and allegiance to the immaculate Imams (a). By loyalty and allegiance we mean truly taking them as role models and following their path to get closer to God. Knowing the Imam without actually following him could actually be detrimental and is simply deviant, because you are responsible for what you know. It is one thing to be de-

---

[18] Al-Kulayni, *Al-Kafi*, 2:38.
[19] Al-Sadouq, *Al-Amaali*, 60.

viant because you are ignorant and it is a whole different level to be deviant while knowing the truth. Furthermore, love on its own is not enough for salvation and guidance either. Loyalty and allegiance needs to follow the knowledge and love for the Imams (a) in order for us to reach the shores of safety. If a person is truly in love then, to the extent of that love, he would automatically follow his beloved and be loyal to them. *"Say, 'If you love God, then follow me; God will love you and forgive you your sins, and God is all-forgiving, all-merciful.'"*[20]

Time and time again, the Holy Prophet (s) emphasized the necessity in paying allegiance and following Ahlulbayt (a) given that they are the ship of salvation and the light of guidance. The Prophet (s) said, *"The example of my household is like that of Noah's Ark. Whoever boards the ark is saved, and whoever falls behind drowns."*[21]

The Holy Prophet (s) also said,

> *Whoever would like to live as I live, die as I die, and enter the eternal paradise that my Lord has promised me, then follow Ali and his progeny after him. They will not lead you away from the gate of guidance, nor will they have you enter into the gate of deviance.*[22]

---

[20] The Holy Quran. Chapter 3 [Arabic: *Aal Imran*]. Verse 31.

[21] Al-Nisabouri, *Al-Mustadrak*, 2:343.

[22] Al-Hindi, *Kanz Al-A'mal*, 6:155.

THE IMAM'S KNOWLEDGE

In the Name of God, the most Beneficent, the most Merciful

Indeed God chose Adam and Noah, and the progeny of Abraham and the progeny of Imran above all the nations; some of them are descendants of the others, and God is all-hearing, all-knowing.[1]

Humanity, in its progression towards God, needs a leader and a guide. God would not leave us without completing His blessings and guidance by providing humanity with divine guides. These are the prophets and messengers (a) that God has blessed us with because of His mercy and compassion – *"God is most kind and merciful to mankind."*[2] At times when no prophets or messengers are sent to the Earth, God still provides us with divine guides. There is no time that the Earth is ever empty of a proof for God. These divine guides play a role of message propagation, guidance, judgment, and governance over the people. They are distinguished by a number of distinct characteristics that allow them to take this noble position. God chooses them only after a process

---

[1] The Holy Quran. Chapter 3 [Arabic: *Aal Imran*]. Verses 33, 34.
[2] The Holy Quran. Chapter 2 [The Cow; Arabic: *Al-Baqara*]. Verse 143.

of trial and testing. When they show their certain beliefs and their patience, they are granted this status. God says, *"When they had been patient and had conviction in Our signs, We appointed amongst them imams to guide [the people] by Our command."*[3] God also says, *"When his Lord tested Abraham with certain words and he fulfilled them, He said, 'I am making you the Imam of mankind.' Said he, 'And from among my descendants?' He said, 'My pledge does not extend to the unjust.'"*[4]

Therefore, the process of choosing these divinely guided leaders was not random or frivolous – God is exalted beyond such petty description. Rather, they were appointed in accordance with the divine will and with divine wisdom after they were tested. Their patience and their certainty allowed them to receive one of the greatest of God's blessings as He gave them what He had not given anyone else. *"And the bounty of your Lord is not confined."*[5]

Amongst the divine blessings that these divinely appointed leaders were given is a divine knowledge different from the knowledge of the rest of mankind. It is narrated that when people pledged allegiance to the Commander of the Faithful (a) as caliph of the Muslim nation, he said in a sermon:

> *Oh people! Ask me before you lose me. Ask me, for I have the knowledge of the first and the last [of mankind]. Surely by God, [if I was given authority to rule over the world] I would judge between the people of Torah by their Torah… Ask me before you lose me, for by the One who has split the seed and created the breeze, if you ask me of any verse I will*

---

[3] The Holy Quran. Chapter 32 [Arabic: *Al-Sajda*]. Verse 24.

[4] The Holy Quran. Chapter 2 [The Cow; Arabic: *Al-Baqara*]. Verse 124.

[5] The Holy Quran. Chapter 17 [The Ascension; Arabic: *Al-Israa*]. Verse 20.

tell you the time of its revelation and the purpose for which it was revealed...[6]

Alongside the rational and scriptural proofs, it is enough of a proof that when cannot find a single instance in history – despite all the distortions that it has went through – where any of our twelve Imams (a) ever stumbled on any question. Even our Imam Jawad (a) who assumed the position of Imam at the age of five was known for his superior intellect and knowledge.

THE NEED FOR THIS STUDY

Some may ask about the need to study this topic. Some may think that it is enough for us to believe that they are the divinely chosen leaders without treading into this discussion. To these objections we answer with the following: believing in the status of our Imams (a) as divinely appointed leaders is the bare minimum level of knowledge that we need to have about them to be able to avoid God's punishment and reach His mercy. Therefore, the more we learn about our Imams (a), the greater the reward – as God says, *"Are those who know equal to those who do not know?"*[7] The benefits of this study are further evidenced in the following points:

Firstly, through further understanding of their status we attain a higher level of belief in them and we allow this faith to take a greater hold of our hearts, as our love for them and awe of them will arise from our knowledge of them. Knowledge allows faith to take root in the human self, so

---

[6] Al-Mufeed, *Al-Irshad*, 23.

[7] The Holy Quran. Chapter 39 [Arabic: *Al-Zumar*]. Verse 9.

that the individual will be able to stand in the way of any misconception, so that he is not led astray by deviant arguments or shaken by seemingly intellectual discussion.

Secondly, greater knowledge of the Imams (a) gives the individual a greater understanding of God and His Oneness. We begin to fully grasp God's greatness. The Imam (a) is a creation and a servant of God. The Imam (a) bears all these traits, perfection, and immaculate nature, yet they all do not equate to even a drop of God's attributes and His infinite perfections. This is one way in which monotheism and belief in God is linked to our Imams (a). The Imams (a) have told us that no one can ever reach true monotheistic belief without them. When Imam Hussein (a) was asked "what is knowing God," he answered, "[it is for] *the people of every era to know their divine leader whom they are obliged to obey.*"

Knowing the Imam is not fulfilled by simply knowing his name and the name of his father. Rather, we need to have a more profound knowledge of the Imam. This is why the Imams (a) have taught us to supplicate with the following words:

> *Oh my God! Allow me to know You, for if you do not allow me to know You I will not know Your Messenger. Oh my God! Allow me to know Your Messenger, for if you do not allow me to know Your Messenger I would not know Your Proof. Oh my God! Allow me to know Your Proof, for if you do not allow me to know Your Proof I will stray away from my religion.*[8]

---

[8] Al-Kulayni, *Al-Kafi*, 1:337.

The knowledge that is being referred to here is not merely general knowledge. We all know that God is our creator, our sustainer, our judge, etc. We all know that His messenger to us is the Prophet Muhammad (s). We all know His proofs on His servants, the first being the Commander of the Faithful Ali ibn Abi Talib (a) and the last being the Imam of Our Time the Awaited Mahdi, peace and blessings be upon him and his fathers. If we were supplicating for the general knowledge alone, then the supplication would be frivolous because we all have this general knowledge. Rather, we are asking for more profound knowledge. That is why it is important to study the attributes of our Imams (a), including their knowledge.

THE NATURE OF THE IMAM'S KNOWLEDGE

Our belief in the knowledge of the Imams (a) is not a novel theory that our scholars have deduced. Rather, it is what our Imams (a) have explicitly taught us since the times of their existence. Their knowledge is unlike the knowledge of any other human. During the time of their presence with the people – about two and a half centuries of time – we do not see any historical reference or claim that anyone asked an Imam of the Holy Household (a) and did not receive a satisfying answer, or that the Imam (a) was hesitant or provided a wrong answer. The greatest challenge to the creed of the followers of the Holy Household (a) came at the time of Imam Jawad (a), who took the position of Imam at the age of five. Shia believers and scholars would follow him and take the teachings of their religion from him.

No one at that time dared to insult the Shia for following someone at such a young age because the people of the time knew of the Imam's (a) knowledge, especially after they saw that he was able to answer any question and debate any scholar in public. Indeed, at one point, the Abbasid ruler, Ma'moon, agreed to allow the Abbasids to test Imam Jawad (a)'s knowledge. Hence, the Abbasids chose one of the most notable scholars of their day to ask Imam al-Jawad an intricate question in Islamic law. After Imam al-Jawad divided the question into eleven distinct subsections, the Abbasid scholar was baffled and began stumbling over his words. At that point, the audience realized the gravity of their false assumption about the young Imam. The Imam (a) then explained the answer to each branch of the original question. Repeated exchanges, such as this one, eliminated the doubts some may have had regarding the superior intellectual merit of Imam Jawad (a).[9]

Imam Baqir (a) said,

> God has general knowledge and specific knowledge. The specific knowledge is that which He has not taught to any of His close angels or His messenger prophets. The general knowledge is that which He taught to His close angels and His messenger prophets. That knowledge came to us through the Messenger of God (s).[10]

It is enough to make mention of the knowledge of our Imams (a) what Sa'id ibn al-Musayyib[11] said: "no one used

---

[9] Al-Beshwaei, *Sirat al-A'immah*, 487-489.

[10] Al-Lari, *Dirasa fi Usus Al-Islam*, 295. Citing, Al-Majlisi, *Bihar Al-Anwar*, 26:160.

[11] Sa'id ibn al-Musayyib. A renowned scholar of Medina and a companion of Imam Sajjad (a).

to say 'ask me [before you lose me]' other than Ali ibn Abi Talib (a)."[12]

THE SOURCES OF THE IMAM'S KNOWLEDGE

The Imams' (a) knowledge comes from a number of sources. These sources are the springs which the Imam (a) drinks from and provides the flow of knowledge to the rest of the believers. We can generally encapsulate the sources of the Imams' (a) knowledge in the following:

The Holy Quran

The major source of the Imams' (a) knowledge is the Holy Quran. One may wonder, "but isn't the Quran a source of learning for all of us?" That's true. However, the Imam (a) has a deep and comprehensive knowledge of the Quran, and we generally need to go through the Prophet (s) and his Household (a) to understand the Quran at a deeper level.

The Imams of the Holy Household (a) are most capable to understand the deep meanings of the Holy Quran and bring out its full potential. As God said, "*We have sent down the Book to you as a clarification of all things and as guidance, mercy and good news for the Muslims.*"[13] However, the individuals that are able to derive the deepest meanings of the Quran are the Holy Household (a). Imam Ali (a) had lived with the Quran moment by moment during its revelation. He learned it from its pure source directly and with all its details. Imam Ali (a) said,

---

12 Al-Ameen, *Aa'yan Al-Shia*, 1:344.
13 The Holy Quran. Chapter 16 [The Bees; Arabic: *Al-Nahl*]. Verse 89.

No verse would be revealed to him [i.e. the Prophet (s)] re-garding night or day, the heavens or the Earth, or this world or the hereafter, except that he would read and dictate it to me. I would write it with my hand. He would teach me its meaning and interpretation, its abrogating and its abro-gated [verses], its precise and its common [verses], its general and its specific, where it is revealed, and why it was revealed until the Day of Judgment.[14]

Imam Ali (a) took the sciences of the Quran directly from the one to whom the Quran was revealed, with all the pre-cise details that surround every verse. This knowledge was not learned by any of the companions of the Prophet (s), nor did anyone of them claim to have such knowledge. This knowledge was transferred from Imam Ali (a) to the im-maculate Imams (a) through the generations.

It is narrated that Imam Sadiq (a) said, *"By God, I know the book of God from beginning to end as though it is all within the palm of my hand. It contains news of the heavens and the earth, and the news of what has occurred and what will occur."*[15]

So the knowledge of the Imams (a) of the Quran is not like any others'. They know the Quran in all of its specificities, parts, and particularities. This is how they have an ability to take from the Holy Quran to the extent far more than any-one else can. That is why the Prophet (s) referred to their significance alongside the Quran when he said, *"I leave amongst you the two weighty things that if you are to hold on to you*

---

14 Al-Harrani, *Tohaf Al-'Oqool*, 196.

15 Al-Kulayni, *Al-Kafi*, 1:229.

would not go astray: The Book of God and my household, my progeny. They will not separate until the reach me at the Pond [of Paradise]."[16]

The Prophetic Heritage

One of the most important sources of the Imams' (a) knowledge is the heritage of their grandfather the Holy Prophet (s). The Prophet (s) paid great attention to the Commander of the Faithful (a) since his youth, and had taught him so much of his knowledge that Imam Ali (a) said, *"The Messenger of God (s) taught me a thousand chapters of knowledge, each of these chapter opens for me another thousand chapters."*[17] The Imam (a) then transferred this knowledge to the succeeding Imams (a). This is why the Imams (a) teach us that all their sayings and teachings go back to the teachings of the Holy Prophet (s). It is narrated that Imam Baqir (a) told Jabir [Al-Ansari],[18]

> *Oh Jabir, if we were to teach based on our opinion and whims, we would have been of the wretched. Rather, we teach from the heritage of the Messenger of God (s). The principles of knowledge are with us. We inherit it from one generation to the next. We treasure it as others treasure their gold and silver.*[19]

Some may object that these narrations are self-praise on the part of the Imams (a). However, they are corroborated by the testimony of other companions and historians. For ex-

---

[16] Al-Majlisi, *Bihar Al-Anwar*, 23:141.

[17] Ibn Shahrashoob, *Al-Manaqib*, 1:315.

[18] Jabir bin 'Abdillah al-Ansari. A companion of the Prophet (s), Imam Ali (a), Imam Hasan (a), Imam Hussein (a), and Imam Sajjad (a). He lived long enough to meet Imam Baqir (a) and take some of his knowledge from him.

[19] Al-Borojourdi, *Jami' Ahadeeth Al-Shia*, 1:130.

ample, we see that Ibn 'Abbas[20] narrates that the Prophet (s) said, *"When I came before my Lord, He spoke to me and conversed with me. I did not learn anything that I would not teach to Ali, as he is the gate to my knowledge."*[21]

Imam Hussein (a) also narrates that when the following verse was revealed, *"We have figured everything in a manifest Imam,"*[22] the companions asked if it was the Torah, the Bible, or the Quran. The Prophet (s) replied *"no."* When Imam Ali (a) approached the Prophet (s), he said, *"this is the Imam in which God figured in knowledge of everything."*[23]

This knowledge that Imam Ali (a) took from the Holy Prophet (s), he wrote it all in a number of books. Imam Ali (a) said,

> *The Messenger of God (s) said, 'Oh Ali, write what I dictate to you.' I said, 'Oh Messenger of God (s), do you fear that I will forget?' He answered, 'No, for I have prayed to God to make you memorize. Rather, you write for your partners.' I asked, 'and who are my partners of Prophet of God?' He said, 'the Imams of your progeny….*[24]

Therefore, what Imam Ali (a) learned from the Prophet (s) was written down and passed along from one Imam to the next. There are tens of narrations that mention this reality.

---

[20] 'Abdallah bin 'Abbas. A companion of the Prophet (s) and disciple of Imam Ali (a). He was a great scholar whom the Prophet (s) prayed for and Imam Ali (a) praised.

[21] Al-Lari, *Dirasa fi Usus Al-Islam*, 295. Citing, Al-Qandouzi, *Yanabee' Al-Mawadda*, 69.

[22] The Holy Quran. Chapter 36 [Arabic: *Yaseen*]. Verse 12.

[23] Al-Lari, *Dirasa fi Usus Al-Islam*, 298. Citing, Al-Qandouzi, *Yanabee' Al-Mawadda*, 77.

[24] Ibid, 302.

That is why we find in some narrations the names of a number of these books, such as Al-Jami'a, the book of Fatima (a), the Book of Ali (a), and others. The Imams (a) go back to these books for clarification of religious teachings, whatever pertains to the people, and the state of the nations and what transpires with them.

Inspiration

Inspiration is another important source of the Imams' (a) knowledge. The Imam (a) has a connection with the unseen world through inspiration, and we have discussed this in an earlier chapter. The issue of inspiration is not a novelty. We sometimes find the most ordinary people inspired at times to deal with certain issues. The Imam (a), who has been given the position of guidance for all mankind, is worthier of this inspiration. It is narrated that Imam Ridha (a) said,

> *If God chooses a servant for handling the matters of His servants, He opens his chest, places in his heart the springs of wisdom, and endows him with knowledge through inspiration. He would not stumble after that on a question and would not be confused away from what is right. He is immaculate, supported, blessed, and reinforced. He is safe from wrong, deviance, and stumbles. God would designate him with this so that he becomes a proof over God's servants and a witness to His creations.* "That is God's grace, which He grants to whomever He wishes, and God is dispenser of a great grace."[25] [26]

[25] The Holy Quran. Chapter 57 [The Iron; Arabic: *Al-Hadeed*]. Verse 21.
[26] Al-Lari, *Dirasa fi Usus Al-Islam*, 302. Citing, Al-Kulayni, *Al-Kafi*, 1:202.

Conversing with the Angels

Another one of the important sources of the Imams' (a) knowledge is conversing with the angels. The problem with discussing this source of knowledge is that whenever it is brought up, we are quickly accused of believing that our Imams (a) are prophets, despite our belief – as all Muslims do – that the Prophet Muhammad (s) is the last prophet and the greatest of all creation.

We do not claim that our Imams (a) are Prophets (s). Rather, we believe that they are a blessing of the blessings of the Grand Prophet (s) – all of their knowledge, honor, and virtue are derived from the Prophet (s).

Let us clarify first that not everyone that converses with angels is a prophet. Angels are creations of God, and they carry out different duties. There are those that harvest the souls, those that ask forgiveness on behalf of the believers, and those that deliver the messages to the prophets, among other roles. We know that the Virgin Mary (a) saw an angel and the angel spoke to her during the Annunciation – when she was given glad tidings that she will give birth to Prophet Jesus (a). We know that at that moment, she had a conversation with the angel, and God relays the story of this conversation in the Holy Quran.

> *And mention in the Book Mary, when she withdrew from her family to an easterly place. Thus did she seclude herself from them, whereupon We sent to her Our Spirit and he became incarnate for her as a well-proportioned human. She*

said, 'I seek the protection of the All-beneficent from you, should you be Godwary!'[27]

Still, despite the fact that she spoke with the angels, no one believes that she was a prophet.

Not all revelation is something that is exclusive to the prophets. There are different types of revelation. One type is specific to the prophets while the others are not. God at times reveals to individuals other than prophets. We see a number of examples of this in the Quran. God says in relating the story of Prophet Moses (a), *"We revealed to Moses' mother, [saying], 'Nurse him; then, when you fear for him, cast him into the river, and do not fear or grieve, for We will restore him to you and make him one of the apostles.'"*[28] Moreover, we see that God provides revelation or divine inspiration for creatures other than humans. God says, *"And your Lord inspired the bee [saying]: Make your home in the mountains, and on the trees and the trellises that they erect."*[29]

Does anyone claim that the mother of Moses (a) was a prophet? Or that bees are prophets? Yet, the Quran specifically tells us that they have received revelations.

The mere fact that the Imams (a) are able to converse with the angels does not make them prophets. Rather, we believe that considering the Imams (a) to be prophets is a form of disbelief in God and His Messenger (s). For, indeed, there is no prophet after Prophet Muhammad (s), the Seal of All Prophets.

---

[27] The Holy Quran. Chapter 19 [Mary; Arabic: *Mariam*]. Verses 16-18.

[28] The Holy Quran. Chapter 28 [The Parables; Arabic: *Al-Qasas*]. Verse 7.

[29] The Holy Quran. Chapter 16 [The Bees; Arabic: *Al-Nahl*]. Verse 68.

We are not the only sect in Islam that says that there are individuals that converse with the angels. The school of thought of the companions also has similar narrations. It is narrated in Sahih Bukhari that Abu Hurayra said, *"The Prophet, may God send his blessings and greetings to him [and his family], said: There was amongst the previous nations of the children of Israel men that would converse [with the angels] without being prophets. If there was any such individual in my nation, it would be Omar."*[30]

I don't know whether there are any Muslims that believe that the men of the Children of Israel are better than the Household of the Prophet Muhammad (s). And if there are individuals in the nation of the Grand Prophet (s) that can converse with the angels, why would this have to exclude the Holy Household (a)? If such talk were to come from followers of other schools of thought, it would be understandable as they do not know the great status of our Immaculate Imams (a). But what excuses do the followers of the School of Thought of the Progeny of the Prophet (s) to deny them these merits?

This is truly astonishing, as Imam Baqir (a) himself has said,

> *I am amazed by some who would pay allegiance to us, believe in our divine guidance, and know that obedience to us is incumbent like obedience of the Messenger of God (s), but they break their testimony and undermine themselves by the weakness of their hearts. They shortchange us on our due right. They mock those who [have given us our due right, those who] God has given the certainty of knowing us and*

---

30 Al-Bukhari, *Sahih Bukhari*, 4:200.

submitting to our command. Do you think that God would obligate His servants with obedience to His vicegerents, and then He would hide from [His vicegerents] the news of the heavens and the earth? And that He would cut off from them the sources of knowledge — knowledge about things that come up which people's faith depends on?[31]

---

[31] Al-Muqarram, *Maqtal Al-Hussein*, 61. Citing, Al-Kulayni, *Al-Kafi*, 1:190. Citing also, Al-Saffar, *Basa'er Al-Darajat*, 33. Citing also: Al-Rawandi, *Al-Kharayij*, 143.

INTERCESSION

In the Name of God, the most Beneficent, the most Merciful

*By the morning brightness, and by the night when it is calm!
Your Lord has neither forsaken you, nor is He displeased
with you, and the Hereafter shall be better for you than the
world. Soon your Lord will give you [that with which] you
will be pleased.[1]*

We are required to live our lives in accordance to what
pleases God in adhering to our religious obligations and
staying within the boundaries of the rules of our religion.
Every deed and every word, big or small, is under God's
observation. Our deeds will be accounted for in accordance
to their quality – reward for good and well-deserved possible punishment for evil.

People may forget about this reality when they are met with
desires and pleasures, and instead will go towards what God
has forbidden. Wouldn't such defiance naturally deserve
God's displeasure, anger, punishment and hellfire? God created all of creation. He is more compassionate to his creation than they are to themselves. God loves them more than

---

[1] The Holy Quran. Chapter 93 [Dawn; Arabic: *Al-Dhuha*]. Verses 1-5.

they love each other. He did not close the gates of mercy before them, nor did he cut off the road of repentance to Him. God is self-sufficient, independent, and in no need; thus, His doors of mercy, repentance and forgiveness remain open. Our worship to God is beneficial only to us and is a mechanism of God's kindness, generosity and mercy towards us. God made seeking forgiveness a door of return, repentance a door of mercy, and intercession a door of hope for the person who falls into wrongdoing. All of these doors are doors to the mercy of God, which has encompassed everything. God opened all of these doors to ensure that humanity will never lose hope in His mercy. *"Indeed no one despairs of God's mercy except the faithless lot."*[2]

THE REALITY OF INTERCESSION AND ITS MEANING

Intercession is the mechanism by which the overflow of God's mercy and forgiveness is received by people through God's vicegerents. God has especially made the request for intercession characteristic for the Day of Judgment. If a person who has made mistakes wishes to return to God, he can ensure his repentance by beseeching God through His vicegerents. The Holy Quran illustrates this with the Holy Prophet (s): *"Had they, when they wronged themselves, come to you and pleaded to God for forgiveness, and the Apostle had pleaded for them [to God] for forgiveness, they would have surely found God all-clement, all-merciful."*[3] In another verse God tells the Prophet (s), *"... and bless them. Indeed your blessing is a comfort to them, and*

---

[2] The Holy Quran. Chapter 12 [Arabic: *Yusuf*]. Verse 87.
[3] The Holy Quran. Chapter 4 [The Women; Arabic: *Al-Nisaa*]. Verse 64.

God is all-hearing, all-knowing."[4] We can see this example in the story of the Jacob's (a) sons after they had committed their crime, were overcome with regret and wanted to return to God. *"They said, 'Father! Plead [with God] for forgiveness of our sins! We have indeed been erring.'"*[5] To that Jacob (a) would reply, *"He said, 'I shall plead with my Lord to forgive you; indeed He is the All-forgiving, the All-merciful.'"*[6]

When we look at some of the other verses in the Quran that discuss the issue of intercession, we may imagine a contradiction with the previous verses. *"Say, 'All intercession rests with God. To Him belongs the kingdom of the heavens and the earth; then you will be brought back to Him.'"*[7] Take the following verse as well

> *Leave alone those who take their religion for play and diversion and whom the life of this world has deceived, and admonish with it, lest any soul should perish because of what it has earned: It shall not have any guardian besides God, nor any intercessor.*[8]

These verses have confined intercession to be with God alone, even though we find many other verses that have given intercession to other than God, specifically God's prophets and vicegerents. To resolve this issue which may seem as a contradiction we have to understand what is meant by intercession in reference to God in the aforementioned verses. The verses here do not infer that God will be

---

[4] The Holy Quran. Chapter 9 [The Repentance; Arabic: *Al-Tawba*]. Verse 103.

[5] The Holy Quran. Chapter 12 [Arabic: *Yusuf*]. Verse 97.

[6] Ibid, Verse 98.

[7] The Holy Quran. Chapter 39 [Arabic: *Al-Zumar*]. Verse 44.

[8] The Holy Quran. Chapter 6 [The Cattle; Arabic: *Al-Anaam*]. Verse 70.

people's intercessor, meaning interceding on their behalf to someone else. Such a statement would be nonsensical for the position of God, because He is the Creator and the Ultimate Judge that people will stand before. Rather, God is the owner of intercession in that no one shall intercede for anyone else except by His permission and approval. Though an individual may have the right to intercede on another's behalf, it is only done by God's consent and authorization. In other words, there is no independent source of influence that exists other than God. Every being's influence – albeit real – is in need of God for its very existence, moment by moment.

Think of water. If we want to quench our thirst, we naturally are inclined to drink water. Water quenches our thirst. Water, however, does not independently quench thirst. God created the system in a way that allowed for certain elements to satisfy and fulfill others, like water to thirst. Without God's will, water could not independently perform that function. This applies to everything, particularly in regards to our discussion of intercession. It is important to keep in mind that the need for God is not only for the initiation of every being's existence, but also for the continuation of every being's existence.

Intercession does not take place except by God's permission. God gave this designation to his vicegerents, the foremost of them being the Leader of Intercedessors and the Mercy to the World Prophet Muhammad (s). The verse, *"Soon your Lord will give you [that with which] you will be pleased."*[9] is speaking of intercession among the things that God will

---

[9] The Holy Quran. Chapter 93 [Dawn; Arabic: *Al-Dhuha*]. Verses 1-5.

give Prophet Muhammad (s). For, regarding this verse, it has been narrated on behalf of Imam Al-Baqir (a) that he would say, *"Intercession. By God intercession, by God intercession."*[10]

THE JUSTIFICATIONS OF INTERCESSION

The following justifications for intercession are examples, not intended to be defining the rational scope of intercession:

Not Being Able to Completely Depend on Action Alone

No matter what people do in pursuit of reaching paradise, they will never reach it on their own. The equation for realizing God's pleasure and contentment and fulfilling one's obligation in submission to God is not so simple. If God were to judge us instantly for our transgressions, very few would be spared. *"Were God to take humans to task because of what they have earned, He would not leave any living being on its back."*[11] When so many are guilty of transgressions, the natural results of their sins cause an effect that impacts all. Even the non-human creatures, which have been created for humans, are thus affected when all humanity is impacted. Who is truly able to fulfill God's right to the complete submission of his creation? Who is able to manifest true thanks for the blessings of God? And who, other than the infallibles, can go throughout their lives without committing grave mistakes, regrettable wrongdoings, and sins that would deserve the punishment of hell? This reality, that we can't rely on

---

[10] Al-Reishahri, *Mizan Al-Hikma*, 2:1041. Citing, Al-Majlisi, *Bihar Al-Anwar*, 8:57.
[11] The Holy Quran. Chapter 35 [Arabic: *Fatir*]. Verse 45.

our deeds alone to be rewarded with paradise, is explained more thoroughly by the narrations from Ahlulbayt (a).

One of the servants of the household of Imam Ali bin Hussain (a), by the name of Aba Ayman, came to Imam Al-Baqir (a) and said, "People are tricked by believing in the intercession of Muhammad (s)." Imam Al-Baqir (a) was angered by his statement replying,

> *Woe to you Aba Ayman! Are you being fooled by [the fact] that you have avoided [sins that are] related to your [carnal desires]? I swear by God that if you were to see the trepidation of the Day of Judgment you would [see your] need for the intercession of Muhammad (s)... this intercession is for those upon whom hellfire has become incumbent.*[12]

Imam Al-Sadiq (a) was asked about the 'believer', and if a believer gets intercession. The Imam (a) responded, *"Yes."* Another question followed up, "Does a believer need the intercession of Muhammad (s)?" The Imam (a) replied, *"Yes, for the believers have mistakes and sins. There is no one that does not need the intercession of Muhammad (s)..."*[13]

Manifesting the Mercy of God

So many of the verses of the Quran illustrate the mercy of God to His creation, for His mercy has encompassed everything. Read the following verse and contemplate on its beauty, *"Say [that God declares,] 'O My servants who have committed excesses against their own souls, do not despair of the mercy of God. Indeed God will forgive all sins. Indeed, He is the All-forgiving, the*

---

12 Al-Subhani, *Fe Thilal Al-Tawheed*, 559. Citing, Al-Barqi, *Al-Mahasin*, 1:183.
13 Ibid, 562.

All-merciful."[14] Our Lord continues to keep the gates of mercy open for us. God Almighty may overlook some of our misdeeds and not disqualify us from the category of "those who do good" so long as it is our character and habit to avoid sins in general. *"Those who avoid major sins and indecencies, excepting [minor and occasional] lapses. Indeed your Lord is expansive in [His] forgiveness. He knows you best..."*[15] Of course, this neither justifies sin nor does it mean that a sinner does not deserve punishment. Rather, it is God's mercy that is emphasized and encourages all to repent to God. However, one must be conscious of God and avoid all sins because it is not about the gravity of the sin as much as it is about the gravity of the One whom we are sinning against – as Prophet Muhammad (s) teaches us.[16]

Furthermore, look at the vastness of God's mercy that He has made one of the jobs of those who surround Him – the greatest of His creation and angels – to pray for the forgiveness for His repenting servants.

> *Those who bear the Throne, and those around it, celebrate the praise of their Lord and have faith in Him, and they plead for forgiveness for the faithful: 'Our Lord! You comprehend all things in mercy and knowledge. So forgive those who repent and follow Your way and save them from the punishment of hell.*[17]

---

[14] The Holy Quran. Chapter 39 [Arabic: *Al-Zumar*]. Verse 53.
[15] The Holy Quran. Chapter 53 [The Star; Arabic: *Al-Najm*]. Verse 32.
[16] Al-Tusi, *Al-Amaali*, 527.
[17] The Holy Quran. Chapter 40 [Arabic: *Ghafir*]. Verse 7.

From these examples we deepen our understanding of intercession as a manifestation of God's ever-flowing mercy to us.

The Honor and Importance of Intercessors

God has chosen from amongst His servants those whose hearts have been tested for faith. Given their ability to hold responsibility, practice patience, with complete certitude, God chose them to fulfill a role that no one else could. They have their honor in this world and in the next. Their significance plays on Earth, in purgatory, and in the afterlife – especially by means of intercession. God honored them with this ability to be the intercessors of people who have fallen into sin and wrongdoing. God is capable of all things. But God has chosen to make the system of forgiveness such that He forgives the believers who have sinned through a system of conditions – the intercessors. In making this system of intercession, God showed the honor and importance of the intercessors.

Through intercession, God honors and shows the noble status of His vicegerents. Intercession allows people to realize the importance of God's vicegerents in their direct connection to salvation with God. Thus, we are naturally inclined to build a better relationship with them in seeking God's pleasure and contentment. Take the example of the Holy Prophet Muhammad (s), the Master of Intercessors, who God told, *"Soon your Lord will give you [that with which] you will be pleased."*[18] In another verse God said, *"And keep vigil for a part of the night, as a supererogatory [devotion] for you. It may be that*

---

[18] The Holy Quran. Chapter 93 [Dawn; Arabic: *Al-Dhuha*]. Verse 5

your Lord will raise you to a praiseworthy station."[19] This 'Praised Station' is intercession.

The Educational Benefits of Intercession

One of the most important effects of intercession is its positive role in educating people; this can be seen in two points:

First, intercession gives hope to those who sin, whereby their faith is reinforced with the idea of intercession and that the doors of God's mercy will not be closed before them. Intercession should not encourage us to commit sins; to the contrary, it should make us more likely to turn to God as we keep hope in His mercy, avoiding the grave sin of despair. It should make us hopeful that we can repent, turn a new page and start fresh, avoiding any future sins. The inexistence of intercession actually could induce one to lose hope and delve deeper into sin God forbid.

Second, in understanding the limits of intercession we see that it is not boundless as believed by some who practiced other schools of thought. Some believed that no matter what sins they committed their prophets or idols would intercede for them on the Day of Judgment. Realizing that intercession has restrictions and is not a free pass to delve into sin makes us more cognizant to reflect over our thoughts and actions. Certain sins may disqualify us from the eligibility to receive certain forms of intercession, God forbid. For example, it has been reported that Imam al-Sadiq (a) said, *"... Indeed, one who takes prayer lightly does not attain our intercession."*[20] If we lose sight of this we will lose grasp of the mer-

---

[19] The Holy Quran. Chapter 17 [The Ascension; Arabic: Al-Israa]. Verse 79.
[20] Al-Kulayni, *Al-Kafi*, 3:270.

cy of intercession that God has generously left open for the believers.

Returning to the Essence of Our Creation

God created us with a sound innate nature that is free from polytheism and deviance. The Holy Quran points to this reality in the following verse, "...*the original nature endowed by God according to which He originated mankind.*"[21] It is also narrated that the Holy Prophet (s) said, "*Everyone is born with the [sound] innate nature. His parents make him Jewish, Christian, or Zoroastrian.*"[22] Sins and wrongdoing are diseases that afflict our innate nature. All the horrors that are witnessed in the grave, at resurrection, and on the Day of Judgment are instruments of treatment to our souls that have become polluted by sin. These events serve as purification for us so that we may return to our natural state of purity and serenity and, if possible, by God's mercy enter heaven. Likewise, intercession has a similar role in providing treatment to our spirits. The intercessors become our doctors, holding our hands as caretakers, and afford treatment to our souls so that we may be cured and enter paradise. In some cases, one's state, due to the person's own exercise of free will, does not qualify for such treatment and requires the treatment of punishment, God forbid. God's mercy is limitless, but if we do not open up for the bare minimum to receive it, we can only blame ourselves. The broadcast of God's mercy is permeating every aspect of existence, but have we made the choice to turn on our receiver?

---

[21] The Holy Quran. Chapter 30 [The Romans; Arabic: *Al-Room*]. Verse 30

[22] Al-Tusi, *Al-Tibyan*, 8:247.

INTERCESSORS ON THE DAY OF JUDGMENT

Our narrations from Ahlulbayt (a) tell us of the intercessors that will intercede on behalf of the believers on the Day of Judgment. Some of them include:

The Holy Quran

God's book will intercede for those who learned it, fulfilled its rights, recited from it and followed it in their lives. Whoever lived by the Quran, not simply memorized or recited its verse, will have it as an intercessor for him on the Day of Judgment. Imam Ali (a) said, *"For whoever the Quran intercedes for on the Day of Judgment, its intercession for him would be accepted."*[23]

Worship and Good Deeds

Acts of worship and good deeds will be among those who intercede for the believers on the Day of Judgment. On that Day, our deeds and actions will take form and become embodied as an intercessor that will testify for us. Thus, it is essential that we do not miss out on the opportunities to increase our good deeds and perform our acts of worship because they hold great weight on the Day of Judgment. It has been reported that Imam Ali (a) said, *"Acting according to righteousness and sticking to honesty are the intercessors for creation."*[24] It is also narrated that the Holy Prophet (s) said, *"The intercessors are five: the Quran, relatives, trusts, your Prophet, and the Household of your Prophet."*[25] Even the smallest of deeds can

---

[23] Al-Radi, *Nahjul Balagha*, 2:92, Sermon 175.

[24] Al-Wasiti, *'Uyoon Al-Hukm wal-Mawa'ith*, 297.

[25] Al-Subhani, *Fe Thilal Al-Tawheed*, 554. Citing, Ibn Shahr Aashoob, *Al-Manaqib*, 2:14.

give a person the right to intercession on the Day of Judgment. Imam Al-Baqir (a) said, *"Whoever walks in the funeral procession of a Muslim will be given four intercessions on the Day of Judgment."*[26]

The Believers

Believers also have the power of intercession on the Day of Judgment, measured based on their level of faith. The more faith a believer has the greater his capacity of intercession will be and the more people he can intercede for. Scholars and martyrs particularly have a great status of intercession. Imam Ali (a) said, *"Three will intercede to God and will be accepted: the Prophets, then the scholars, and thereafter the martyrs."*[27] It is also narrated that the Holy Prophet (s) said, *"The least of the believers will be able to intercede for forty of his brothers."*[28]

The Prophet and his Household

The greatest intercessor on the Day of Judgment is the Holy Prophet (s). We mentioned previously narrations that point to the station of the Prophet (s) and his Household (a) in regards to intercession. The Messenger of God (s) said, *"I will intercede on the Day of Judgment and my intercession will be accepted. Ali (a) will intercede and his intercession will be accepted. My Household will intercede and their intercession will be accepted."*[29]

There is a particular intercessor from within the Household of the Prophet (s) that has a special intercession – Lady Fat-

---

[26] Ibid, 558. Citing, Al-Tusi, *Al-Tahtheeb*, 4:455.

[27] Ibid, 555. Citing, Al-Sadouq, *Al-Khisal*, 156.

[28] Ibid, 488. Citing, Al-Mufeed, *Awa'il Al-Maqalat*, 80.

[29] Ibn Shahr Aashoob, *Al-Manaqib*, 2:15; Al-Tabrasi, *Mujamma' Al-Bayan*, 1:202.

ima (a). God has separated those who love Fatima (a) from the fire of hell. It is narrated that Imam Al-Baqir (a) said:

> On the Day of Judgment, Fatima (a) will have a stand on the gate of hell. On that Day every person will have written on his forehead, 'believer' or 'disbeliever'. A person who loves [Fatima (a)] but has committed an abundance of sin will be ordered to hell. Fatima will read 'lover' on his forehead and say: 'My Lord and Master, You have named me Fatima and through me you have separated those who followed me and my progeny from hellfire. And Your promise is the truth and You never break Your promises.' God replies, 'You have told the truth O' Fatima. I have named you Fatima and through you I have separated those who love and follow you and your progeny from hellfire. And my promise is the truth, and I do not break my promises. I have ordered this servant of mine to hellfire so that you may intercede for him, and I will accept your intercession. That way my angels, prophets, messengers, and the people of the stand [for judgment], see your position [of esteem] to Me and your status [in my eyes]...[30]

DEPRIVED FROM INTERCESSION

There are some, however, that are deprived of the intercession of Muhammad (s) and his Household (a). Some of them are included below:

The Disbeliever

A person who has inexcusably abandoned faith cannot receive the intercession of any intercessor. How could one

---

[30] Al-Majlisi, *Bihar Al-Anwar*, 8:51.

who has sealed his own heart and rejected submission to God and the guardianship of God receive intercession? Heaven is quintessentially forbidden for the inexcusable disbeliever who does not repent. The Holy Quran mentions the inability of disbelievers to benefit from intercession, *"[They would say,] 'we used to deny the Day of Retribution until death came to us.' So the intercession of the intercessors will not avail them."*[31] The Holy Prophet (s) also said, *"Intercession is not for the people of doubt and polytheism, nor for the people of disbelief and ingratitude; rather, it is only for the believers from the people of monotheism."*[32] Therefore, we must take heed from falling into ascribing partners to God and disbelief, God forbid. Some sins can lead a person to surrender his faith and follow the path of disbelief; should that occur, then no intercession will help him nor can he be from those who God is content with.

The Enemies of Ahlulbayt

Such individuals have exceeded every level of wrongdoing where it is impossible for them to receive intercession. Imam Ali (a) said, *"The Holy Prophet (s) said, 'Standing at the Praised Station I will [even] intercede for those of my nation who have committed the greater sins and God will accept my intercession. But by God, I will not intercede for those who have harmed my progeny."*[33] How could one who is an enemy of Muhammad's (s) progeny expect to receive intercession from Muhammad (s)? Note that if a person was content with the harm done to

---

[31] The Holy Quran. Chapter 74 [Arabic: *Al-Muddathir*]. Verses 46-48.

[32] Al-Reyshahri, *Mizan Al-Hikma*, 2:1472. Citing, Al-Majlisi, Bihar Al-Anwar, 8:58.

[33] Al-Subhani, *Fe Thilal Al-Tawheed*, 556. Citing, Al-Sadouq, *Al-Amaali*, 370.

Ahlulbayt (a) by their enemies, that person is considered a partner in that act of evil. Imam Al-Sadiq (a) said, "*A believer can intercede for his close ones, unless he is an enemy [of Ahlulbayt]. If every prophet and angel were to intercede for an enemy [of Ahlulbayt] their intercession would not be accepted.*"[34] The Prophet (s) promises the exact opposite of this for the lovers of his progeny. He is narrated to have said, "*I am the intercessor for four on the Day of Judgment: the one who has shown generosity to my progeny after me, the one who fulfills their needs, the one who strives to help them when they need him, and the one who loves them with his heart and tongue.*"[35]

The Person Who Neglects His Prayer

This act of worship is so significant it is considered to be the pillar of religion as related to us by some of our narrations. One of the companions of Imam Al-Sadiq (a), Abu Baseer, visited the Imam's (a) wife Um Hameeda to pay condolences after the martyrdom of the Imam (a). He found her crying and thus cried with her. She said,

> *If you were to see Aba Abdillah (a) at his death you would be bewildered. He opened his eyes and said, 'Gather all those that are close to me.' So we did not leave anyone that we knew except that we gathered them. He looked at them and said, 'Our intercession does not reach one who takes prayer lightly.*'[36]

---

[34] Ibid, 550. Citing, Al-Sadouq, *Thawab Al-'Amal*, 251.

[35] Ibid, 464. Citing, Al-Sadouq, *'Uyoon Akhbar Al-Rida*, 2:230.

[36] Ibid, 484. Citing, Al-Amili, *Al-Wasael*, 3:16.

The One Who Denies the Intercession of the Messenger of God

Those who deny the intercession of the Holy Prophet (s) will not be privileged to receive his intercession. (s). The Prophet (s) said, "*Whoever does not believe in my intercession then may God not give him my intercession.*"[37] He also said, "*My intercession on the Day of Judgment is a truth, for whoever does not believe in it he will not be from [those who receive it].*"[38] Also narrated from Imam Ali (a), "*Whoever denied the intercession of the Messenger of God, will not receive it.*"[39]

---

[37] Al-Reyshahri, *Mizan Al-Hikma*, 2:1472. Citing, Al-Majlisi, *Bihar Al-Anwar*, 8:34.

[38] Ibid. Citing, Al-Hindi, *Kanzal A'mal*, 14:399.

[39] Ibid. Citing, Al-Majlisi, *Bihar Al-Anwar*, 8:40.

PREPARING FOR
THE REAPPEARANCE

In the Name of God, the most Beneficent, the most Merciful

He is the One who sent His Messenger with guidance and the religion of truth, that He might cause it to prevail over all religions, though the polytheists may be averse.[1]

The 15th of Sha'ban marks the day that the twelfth Imam of Ahlulbayt (a) was born – Imam Al-Mahdi (aj). Through this Imam, God will fulfill His promise of manifesting His religion, His justice, and His message – the message of Muhammad (s) – throughout the world. God repeated this promise in two different chapters of the Quran as a clear statement and emphasis of this divine promise. God mentioned it a third time and ended the verse with "*...and God is enough for a witness.*"[2] The meaning of this, according to some scholars, is that God is the one who promised and God is the one that will witness the manifestation of His promise. A witness other than God is prone to mistake, forgetful-

---

[1] The Holy Quran. Chapter 9 [The Repentance; Arabic: *Al-Tawba*]. Verse 33.
[2] The Holy Quran. Chapter 48 [The Victory; Arabic: *Al-Fath*]. Verse 28.

ness, heedlessness or ignorance; God is not. Thus, He is the best to promise and the best to witness His promise come to fruition.[3]

There is no disagreement between the schools of thought regarding the belief that God will fill the Earth with justice and equality after it has been filled with injustice, oppression and ignorance. Humanity will be blessed with stability, peace, and justice as opposed to the many years that man oppressed and harmed his fellow man. Thus, this discussion is extremely relevant and affects each and every one of us. More specifically, in this chapter we are discussing the necessity of waiting for the Reappearance of Imam al-Mahdi (a) and preparing for the day that humanity will witness a drastic transformation in its relationship with God and the relationships between people. That day God's divine law will be realized in its totality and specificity. This could be described as the final era of human history. *"And We desired to bestow a favor upon those who were deemed weak in the land, and to make them the Imams, and to make them the heirs."*[4]

In this discussion ask yourself the following questions:

- What is our position in regards to this tremendous world-changing event?
- What are the instruments needed in this role?

OUR POSITION REGARDING THE REAPPEARANCE

There is a phrase that is used by logicians and jurists, and that is, that a proposed notion's relation to another can be

---

[3] Al-Jaafari, *Al-Ghayba*, 25.
[4] The Holy Quran. Chapter 28 [The Parables; Arabic: *Al-Qasas*]. Verse 5.

described in one of the following terms: positively contingent, negatively contingent or non-contingent. Take prayer as an example. Prayer in regards to ablution is positively contingent, which means that the prayer would not be correct with being pure via the ablution. The prayer is contingent on something, the ablution. Now consider the relationship between prayer and eating. Here there exists a negative contingency, which means that in order for the prayer to be correct you *cannot* eat while in prayer. Thus, the prayer is contingent upon the negation of eating – not eating. Finally, consider the relationship between prayer and the type of clothing you wear. We are not required to wear specific color, brand or material of clothing in our prayer. Thus, prayer in this aspect is non-contingent.

After understanding this concept, we can ask ourselves the following: which one of the states describes our relationship to the issue of the reappearance of Imam Al-Mahdi (aj)? Is it a positive contingency, negative contingency or non-contingent? In other words, does God expect us to take a specific position regarding the Imam's (a) reappearance such that his reappearance is contingent upon something happening? Or are we required to not take any specific position and instead remain quiet and wait until he reappears to clarify our religious obligation – which is essentially then a negative contingency? Or could it be that our narrations from Ahlulbayt (a) are silent on this matter and thus we have a choice in taking a position or not taking a position, making this issue apparently non-contingent?

When we go back to the narrations of Ahlulbayt (a) we find that the topic of reappearance requires action in a few aspects; thus, it falls within the category of positive contingency from that viewpoint.

WHAT IS THE REQUIRED STANCE OF A PERSON IN THE TIME OF OCCULTATION?

Amongst the narrations of Ahlulbayt (a), there are some narrations that are more well-known than others. These narrations are characteristic in describing awaiting 'the relief' – the reappearance of the Imam (aj).

The Commander of the Faithful (a) said, "*Await the relief and do not lose hope in God, for the dearest act to God is awaiting the relief.*"[5] It is also narrated that when Imam Al-Sadiq (a) was listing the characteristics of true faith he said, "*Devotion, chastity, righteousness... and awaiting the relief with patience.*"[6]

We can interpret 'awaiting the relief' or 'awaiting the reappearance' in two ways:

The First View: In the era of occultation, we are not to engage in anything that is incompatible with waiting, whether it be engaging in the good or forbidding the evil. Nor should we initiate any social change that is aimed at bringing reform for the community or the nation. Some people in this camp go to the extent to believe and propagate the necessity of spreading corruption, because in their twisted belief the more corruption spreads in the world the faster the reappearance will come. They believe that the Imam (aj) will not reappear until the Earth is completely plagued by corruption and immorality.

---

[5] Al-Sadr, *Tareekh Al-Ghayba Al-Kubra*, 321.
[6] Ibid.

Even though some hold this view, this outlook on 'awaiting the relief' is perverse, erroneous, and the farthest possible perspective on what it truly means to await the reappearance.

The Second View: In awaiting the Imam (aj), we are supposed to ready ourselves and prepare for his arrival and the day that has been promised by God. In anticipation of a guest or a relative that will be paying a visit to your house, do you not make sure that every aspect of the home is prepared so that you can welcome your guest in the proper way? Naturally, we make sure that the house is clean, the dishes are washed, there is food and drink to offer the guest, and that the house is a place that our guest will feel welcome in. You take care of these preparations before your guest arrives, not when they knock on the door. How embarrassed would we be if a visitor were to knock, knowing that they would come at any time, but you did not make an effort to prepare for their arrival? In the same way, waiting for the Imam (aj) requires us to prepare for his arrival so that when he does arrive we are able to serve him and properly join him.

The Imam (aj) will come at a time known to no other but God. It is narrated that someone asked the Holy Prophet (s), "O' Messenger of God, when will the savior from your progeny rise?" The Prophet (s) would respond, "*His [situation regarding the time of his rise] is analogous to the [situation regarding the] Time [of the Day of Judgment]. Only God knows when it will be...*"[7] Therefore, we must make our most diligent effort to prepare for him in every possible moment of our lives. If

---

[7] Al-Qummi, *Kifayet Al-Athar*, 277.

we do not, we are likely to be caught off guard and even shocked by the Imam's (aj) reappearance.

THE WAYS TO PREPARE FOR THE REAPPEARANCE

What are the essential methods and ways that we can follow whereby we are considered as people awaiting the Imam (aj) and preparing for his reappearance?

Adhering to the Line of the Great Maraji' (Jurists)

God's wisdom dictated that He would guide people and counsel them to the true righteous path by sending prophets and messengers. After the prophets and the messengers God sent vicegerents as the leaders of truth guiding people to His path. The vicegerents take people by the hand and lead them to their Lord. Sometimes people see how the vicegerents exercise their role, and at other times the role of the vicegerents – albeit present and necessary – is covert or hidden from the people. In the era of occultation (when the Imam's identity is hidden), this same proof of God must exist. There must be someone who bears this proof upon the people and is ready to clarify to them what their obligations and duties are. God can provide such an individual and because He is so Kind, He definitely does provide such an individual. But because of the problems people make, in order to protect this vicegerent or for other possible wisdoms, God may command the vicegerent to keep his identity hidden from people in certain circumstances. In such circumstances, the Imam (aj) continues to play his role to the greatest extent possible.

The Imam (aj) made the scholars the proof upon people so that we may follow them in his absence. They are his proof upon the people and he, the Imam (aj), is God's proof. *"In your current affairs go back to the narrators of our traditions [i.e. the jurists], for they are my proof upon you and I am God's proof."*[8] In regards to the jurists and their authority, it is narrated that Imam Al-Sadiq (a) said,

> ... *Let them be content with them as judges, for I have made them an authority over you. So if they rule in accordance to our rule, and people do not accept their verdict then the people are belittling the verdict of God. In that, they dispute our authority, and those who dispute our authority dispute the authority of God – and that is equal to ascribing a partner to God.*[9]

It is essential that we emphasize the importance of choosing our *Marja'* (jurist to follow) properly. Our decision should not be based on emotion or whim. This issue is not arbitrary for a person to choose based on what appeals to them. Rather, there is a set of qualifications that a person must look at like knowledge, justice, credentials, and other matters that are listed as the requirements of being a *Marja'*. To have nationalism, love, hatred, ethnocentrism or any other affiliation be considered in one's decision of who to follow when someone else is more qualified, that is completely unacceptable. In such a case, a person's actions risk being null and void! The likes of such a situation is analogous to the state of those who would only accept from their prophets the things that they liked. When a prophet was not in line

---

[8] Al-Tusi, *Al-Ghayba*, 176; Al-Amili, *Wasael Al-Shia*, 18:101.

[9] Al-Amili, *Wasael Al-Shia*, 18:98.

with their whims, they rejected and sometimes even killed their prophets:

> *And most certainly We gave Musa the Book and We sent apostles after him one after another; and We gave Isa, the son of Mariam, clear arguments and strengthened him with the holy spirit, What! whenever then an apostle came to you with that which your souls did not desire, you were insolent so you called some liars and some you slew.*[10]

Thus, it is not a legitimate excuse for a person who has learned of the requirements of following a jurist to choose not to follow simply because they don't 'connect' with the jurist. In other words, you should not follow a jurist because he fits within your political, social or economic ideology. If we cannot follow our jurists because we are unable to shift from our fallible preconceived notions, habits, or already established outlooks, then how do we expect to follow our Imam (aj) once he reappears? The Imam (aj) will come to elevate humanity above invalid traditions, customs, and beliefs. He will bring reform to what many have held to be part and parcel of their ideologies and worldviews. The inability to follow a jurist based on the proper qualifications and prerequisites will result in a greater likelihood of deviance when the Awaited Imam (aj) reappears.

Building Our Spirituality and Creed

Preparing for the reappearance of the Imam (aj) requires us to develop ourselves spiritually and theologically. The Imam (aj) needs supporters who are strong in their creed, ethics,

---

[10] The Holy Quran. Chapter 2 [The Cow; Arabic: *Al-Baqara*]. Verse 87.

and abilities that can only be fortified by building one's spirituality through learning the teachings of the religion.

The noble narrations describe this group of supporters for Imam Al-Mahdi (aj). There is a specific narration from Imam Hussain (a) regarding the Mahdi (aj) that says,

> *The people of the era of the [Mahdi's] occultation who believe in his leadership and await his reappearance are better than the people of any era. This is because God gave them intellect, understanding, and knowledge that caused the occultation to be for them as if they see [the Imam]. And God made the people of that era at the status of the warriors of the Holy Prophet (s). They are truly the sincere ones... and call to [the way of] God in secret and in the open.*[11]

Sheikh Al-Tusi also narrates that the Holy Prophet (s) said, *"There will be a people after you, that one of their men's reward [for his deeds] will be worth the reward for fifty of your men."* Those around him replied, "O' Messenger of God, we were with you in the Battles of Badr, Uhud, Hunayn, and the Quran was revealed to us..." The Prophet (s) then said, *"If you were to bear what they bear, you would not have their patience."*[12]

True preparation translates into a person feeling a greater responsibility in the era of occultation to build a strong righteous community. It means that we engage in the good and forbid the evil. It means that we discipline, develop and advance ourselves in our creed and ethics. By being in this mindset and state of living, it will help us better receive the vast changes and reform the Imam (aj) will make when he

---

[11] Al-Sadr, *Tareekh Al-Ghayba Al-Kubra*, 377. Citing, Al-Sadouq, *Ikmal al-Din*, 32.
[12] Ibid.

reappears. Our narrations tell us that the great social and ideological reforms that the Imam (aj) will bring forth will not be readily accepted by those who are not firm in their faith in God. Like the era of occultation, the era of reappearance will also witness instigation and sedition. Thus, only the ones that absorbed deeply into their religion and their true faith in God will overcome such challenges, understand the reforms of the Imam (aj) and support him in his movement.

A person who is weak spiritually and theologically is less likely to accept the actions of the Imam (aj) and may actually begin to doubt his leadership when he does reappear. That is why it is essential to develop one's spirituality and understanding in creed, because it makes an individual strong in facing the hardships, challenges, and ridicule during the time of occultation. Those who have not developed such a foundation may be weak and prone to lose hope in the Imam (aj). Such a person may even doubt the reappearance of the Imam (aj) and misconceptions may begin take a toll on his heart.

Not Being Tied Down to this World and Material Attachments

To be effective in preparing for the Imam (aj), we need to avoid being attached to the world and materialism. These things could be a cause for our drift from the cause of the Imam (aj). He will come to create the greatest reform witnessed by mankind – we need to be ready to support that with all our time and resources. Having unhealthy attachments to money, entertainment, family, children, and affluence are obstacles in joining the Imam's (aj) movement.

This is a reality that people before us have faced, and the Holy Quran discusses it in the following verse:

> *O you who believe! What (excuse) have you that when it is said to you: Go forth in God's way, you should incline heavily to earth; are you contented with this world's life instead of the hereafter? But the provision of this world's life compared with the hereafter is but little.*[13]

The more things we are unhealthily attached to in this material world, the more difficult sacrifice will be. A person could be prevented from following the Imam (aj) because of his inability to sacrifice what he has become deeply attached to. Our attachments could be the reason for us even standing against the Imam (aj). What would our position be if the Imam (aj) told us to give up our wealth because we don't have a right to it? Or what if he were to tell us to disown some of the people that are dear to us because they are not on the path of truth? What would we do if he ordered us to practice something that we felt was too difficult in following his orders? Think of your attachments and see how they could possibly be a cause for your lack of subordination for the Imam (aj). To be disobedient to the immaculate Imam (aj) is to be disobedient to the Prophet (s) and to God Almighty Himself..

---

[13] The Holy Quran. Chapter 9 [The Repentance; Arabic: *Al-Tawba*]. Verse 38.

FANATICISM

In the Name of God, the most Beneficent, the most Merciful

It does not behoove any human that God should give him the Book, judgement and prophethood, and then he should say to the people, 'Be my servants instead of God.' Rather [he would say], 'Be a godly people, because of your teaching the Book and because of your studying it.' And he would not command you to take the angels and the prophets for lords. Would he call you to unfaith after you have submitted [to God]?[1]

We have discussed in the previous chapters the great status and proximity to God that our Grand Prophet (s) and his Immaculate Household (a) attained. After those chapters, some may come out and ask, "isn't this status that you have given to the Prophet (s) and the Holy Household (a) excessive? Aren't we being fanatics in this regard?"

It is narrated that Imam Sadiq (a) narrates from his forefathers saying, "*The Messenger of God (s) said: do not praise me*

---

[1] The Holy Quran. Chapter 3 [Arabic: *Aal Imran*]. Verses 79, 80.

above my right, for God has taken me as a servant before taking me as a prophet."²

It is also narrated that Imam Ali (a) said, "*Beware of fanaticism regarding us. Say that we are servants of [the] Lord, and then say of our merits what you wish.*"³

THE RELIGIOUS RULING REGARDING FANATICISM

There are many narrations that prohibit fanaticism. It is narrated that Imam Sadiq (a) said,

> *Beware for your youth of the fanatics so that they do not corrupt them. The fanatics are the worst of God's creation. They minimize God's glory and call for deification of His servants...*⁴

There are many similar narrations from the Household of the Prophet (s) that hold the same meaning. From such traditions, some of our scholars have deduced that the fanatic is counted in the ranks of the disbelievers. But in response to this clear deviance, the scholars of the school of thought of the Holy Household (a) have taken a strong stance against fanaticism. Despite this stance, we still see in the books of our scholars traditions that describe the merits and the miracles of our Immaculate Leaders (a); these traditions may appear to some to be fanatical. Why would our scholars include such traditions in their books? If these traditions were truly fanatical, our scholars would have surely rejected

---

² Al-Rawandi, *Al-Nawadir*, 125.

³ Al-Sadouq, *Al-Khisal*, 614.

⁴ Al-Tusi, *Al-Amaali*, 650.

them. The answer can be found in understanding the meaning of fanaticism.

THE MEANING OF FANATICISM

Fanaticism lies in crossing the boundaries and ascribing to creations attributes that they cannot possess. To further understand this definition, we must go back to the narrations that describe to us a number of examples of fanaticism.

Deification

It is narrated the Imam Sadiq (a) said, "*A man once came to the Messenger of God (s) and said, 'peace be upon you, oh my lord.' The Prophet (s) said, 'what is wrong with you? May God distance you from his mercy. Your Lord and my Lord is God.*"[5] Imam Ali (a) also said, "*Beware of fanaticism regarding us. Say that we are servants of a Lord....*"[6] It's also narrated that the Imams (a) have cursed a number of individuals for being fanatics, such as Aba Al-Khattab and others.

Absolute Delegation

Those who believe in absolute delegation say that God created all of creation then left it all up to the Imams (a) to do with it as they wish, so that they pass blessings to whomever they wish, give life to whomever they wish, and send death upon whomever they wish, independent of God. This is impossible and is a clear form of ascribing partners to God. As Imam Ridha (a) said, "*the fanatics are disbelievers and [those who believe in absolute delegation] are polytheists.*"[7] It is also narrat-

---

[5] Al-Tusi, *Ikhtiyar Ma'rifat Al-Rijaal*, 2:589.

[6] Al-Sadouq, *Al-Khisal*, 614.

[7] Al-Sadouq, *'Uyoon Akhbar Al-Rida*, 2:219.

ed that when one of the companions of Imam Sadiq (a) told him of a man who held this belief, Imam Sadiq (a) said,

> *The enemy of God is lying. If you were to go back to him read him this verse from the chapter of The Thunder:* 'Have they set up for God partners who have created like His creation, so that the creations seemed confusable to them? Say, "God is the creator of all things, and He is the One and the All-paramount.*"[8]...[9]*

Ascribing Prophethood to them

The Imams (a) have prohibited us from ascribing prophethood to them, as that would be a form of disbelief in God and His Messenger (s), the final prophet. It is narrated that Imam Sadiq (a) said, *"Whoever says that we are prophets, may God distance him from His mercy. Whoever is doubtful of that, may God distance him from His mercy."*[10]

Calling to Disobedience of God

This is clear in the narration of Imam Sadiq (a) that we mentioned earlier, in which he says, *"Beware for your youth of the fanatics so that they do not corrupt them..."* [11] as those fanatics will call for people toward deviant beliefs and justify abandoning prayers, fasting, alms, and the pilgrimage.

---

[8] The Holy Quran. Chapter 13 [The Thunder; Arabic: *Al-Ra'd*]. Verse 16.

[9] Al-Sadouq, *Al-I'tiqadat fi Deen Al-Imamiyya*, 100.

[10] Al-Majlisi, *Bihar Al-Anwar*, 25:296.

[11] Al-Tusi, *Al-Amaali*, 650.

RE-EXAMINING THE TRADITIONS

After we have understood the true meaning of fanaticism, we can go back and examine the narrations of the merits and the miracles of the Holy Household (a). But before we do, let us first point out the gravity of the issue of fanaticism. Fanaticism is not a mere empty word that can be thrown at any scholar, lecturer, or author. We must understand the gravity of the word when we use it. When we describe someone as a fanatic, we are claiming that they have renounced belief in the Oneness of God, the Exalted, and ascribed others as partners to Him.

We must be careful in describing any narration of the Holy Household (a) as fanatical. If we erroneously make such an accusation, we are in danger of falling into the following sins:

- discrediting their true words, which is equivalent to rejecting God's words (this equates to a rejection of the faith, as anyone who rejects the words of God has rejected the faith);
- Falsely accusing a great number of religious scholars of being fanatics, due to one's ignorance and lack of understanding that they are not at all fanatical.

So what do we do with narrations that we cannot comprehend?

It is narrated that Imam Sadiq (a) said,

> By God, the most beloved to me of my companions is the most pious, knowledgeable, and cautious in relaying our traditions. The worst in status and most abhorrent are those

that if they hear a tradition that is credited to us and [was not willing to accept it] he would be disgusted, reject it, and consider whoever has faith in it a disbeliever, while he does not know [the truth of it.] Perhaps that tradition did come from us and is related back to us. In [rejecting as such], he would be outside [the scope of] allegiance to us.[12]

In another narration, a man comes to Imam Sadiq (a) and asks about such narrations that may seem far-fetched to some at first glance. The man complains that some narrations are so difficult to believe that he may be driven to accuse the narrator of lying. The Imam (a) asks *"is he not attributing what he tells you to me?"* The man would reply yes. Imam Sadiq (a) would then ask, *"does he call the night day and the day night?"* – meaning does he speak anything that is obviously wrong and logically impossible? The man would answer no. The Imam (a) would then say, *"refer it to us, for if you [consider it a lie] then you are rather [considering us to be lying]."*[13] By telling the man *"refer it to us,"* Imam Sadiq (a) is instructing us that when we come across such a narration, we should not consider it a lie right off the bat. As long as there is a possibility that it is true, even if we don't understand it completely yet, the Imams (a) may have said it and surely have the explanation for it.

When the narration's content is questionable or debatable, it is very important to ask the scholar, lecturer, or author in question about the source of the narration. When we go back to the source, we are able to examine its chain of narrators. We can also, then, aim to understand its meaning

---

[12] Al-Kulayni, *Al-Kafi*, 2:223.

[13] Al-Saffar, *Basa'er Al-Darajat*, 558.

from the context and by reviewing scholarly commentaries. Asking these questions will more likely lead us to the correct answer. If a person cannot come to a conclusion about these narrations, he should not reject them, especially since he is not a scholar and an expert in the field. When a person allows for unmethodical doubts to reverberate in one's heart, God forbid it may eventually lead to belying something that is actually true. Not having the answer right away does not warrant such harmful doubts. There is room for healthily referring the content back to those who know when we do not know.

We should not pay heed to those who mock us for our belief in our Imams (a). If we have certain belief in our creed, their mockery will not affect us. People have mocked the prophets before us. The Prophet Noah (a), for example, was ridiculed for building an ark where there is no sea. But once the command of God became visible to all, everyone knew who is the reasonable and who is the heedless.

DEATH

And they used to say, 'What! When we are dead and become dust and bones, shall we be resurrected?! And our forefathers too?!' Say, 'Indeed the former and latter generations will all be gathered for the tryst of a known day.'[1]

INTRODUCTION

We will attempt to highlight a host of fundamental points that the topic builds on, including;

First: The human is the axis of this universe, and everything in the universe, is at his disposal. God favored the human over most of the other creations. Rather, he is the best creation due to the special nature and abilities he possesses that are not found in other creations. The Holy Quran emphasized the reality of the special abilities and status of the human being in a multitude of verses such as in the verse,

---

[1] The Holy Quran. Chapter 56 [Arabic: *Al-Waqia*]. Verse 47-50.

Do you not see that God has disposed for you whatever there is in the heavens and whatever there is in the earth and He has showered upon you His blessings, the outward, and the inward? Yet among the people are those who dispute concerning God without any knowledge or guidance or an illuminating scripture.[2]

In another verse God states, *"He has disposed for you[r benefit] whatever is in the heavens and whatever is on the earth; all is from Him. There are indeed signs in that for a people who reflect."*[3]

There are other verses that refer to man's ability to control a host of natural forces that are put under his command such as the mountains and winds, and Prophet Suleiman's command over birds and the Satanic forces. For the human is the focal point of this universe and the best of creation, which God willed to put all of his other creation under his command and to grant him a great responsibility to be God's vicegerent. In other words, the human must attain a high status of ascension, knowledge, and realization so that he is able to fulfill that responsibility and be worthy of it.

Second: The Islamic perspective on life indicates that the human life was not created to simply cease to exist, but rather to remain everlasting so that it can accomplish the divine vision. That vision is for the human to benefit from all of creation and worship God Almighty. There are numerous religious texts that speak to this understanding and emphasize this reality. The Commander of the Faithful (a) is narrated to have said *"Oh people, you and us have been created to remain and not to cease to exist. Rather, you are transported from one*

---

[2] The Holy Quran. Chapter 31 [Arabic: *Luqman*]. Verse 20.

[3] The Holy Quran. Chapter 45 [Arabic: *Al-Jathiya*]. Verse 13.

*home to another. So attain provisions for that which you are heading
towards and will remain in forever.*"[4]

There is another religious text narrated by Masada Bin
Ziyad who said,

> *A man told Jaafer Ibn Muhammed (a), oh Aba Abd Al-
> lah, we have been created for something astonishing. The
> Imam (a) asked,* 'what would that be?' *The man an-
> swered, we have been created in order to cease to exist. The
> Imam (a) answered,* 'slow down brother for we have
> been created to continue to exist. How can a para-
> dise that doesn't wither and a fire that does not
> subside cease to exist? Rather, we travel from one
> home to another.*"[5]

Third: A human being lives in this life only for a number of
years and then dies. Is that it? Is there nothing beyond?
With humanity's amazing potential, and the Wisdom of the
Merciful Lord, can the human soul's journey simply end
with physical death? Without a life beyond this life, the system of creation would be futile. To live merely to die is
meaningless. Would the Wise Lord create a being, especially
one with such potential, merely to die? Of course not. This
is what the Holy Quran pointed to in the verse *"Did you suppose that We created you aimlessly, and that you will not be brought
back to Us?"*[6]

Fourth: The afterlife that a human being experiences is
much vaster compared to than this worldly physical life. No

---

[4] Al-Tusi, *Al-Amaali*, 1:216.

[5] Al-Majlisi, *Bihar Al-Anwar*, 5:313.

[6] The Holy Quran. Chapter 23 [The Believers; Arabic: *Al-Mu'minoon*]. Verse 115

matter how long a person lives in this world, these years are minor in comparison to the life that awaits one beyond physical death. The eventual life beyond is either an eternal bliss or an eternal punishment.

Fifth: The aforementioned draws attention to the significance of being concerned with the lives and worlds that await the human being. Generally, humanity expends most of its focus on knowing the secrets of this world and what leads to the happiness of man in it. But they generally do not focus nearly as much on the next life, even though this life is not but a life of play and amusement compared to the eternal life. As is stated in the Holy Quran, *"The life of this world is nothing but diversion and play, but the abode of the Hereafter is indeed Life (itself), had they known!"*[7]

Islam gave the issues of eternal life significant attention and stressed that it is imperative on the believer to pay attention to it and understand his place in it. Similar to how one works tirelessly in this life to attain positions that will result in happiness and satisfaction, he must pay attention to the eternal life and strive to attain the positions that will earn him happiness and satisfaction. There is no doubt that the eternal life takes precedence over this life. *"And the Hereafter shall be better for you than the world."*[8]

A key feature of a believer is his concern with the eternal life. The believer strives to attain the high status in it, as opposed to the non-believer who does not see but this world as his primary concern and worry. He does not work but for

---

[7] The Holy Quran. Chapter 29 [The Spider; Arabic: *Al-Ankabout*]. Verse 64.

[8] The Holy Quran. Chapter 93 [Dawn; Arabic: *Al-Dhuha*]. Verse 4.

this world and does not desire but to know the means to attain it. God states,

> *Whoever desires this transitory life, We expedite for him*
> *therein whatever We wish, for whomever We desire. Then*
> *We appoint hell for him, to enter it, blameful and spurned.*
> *Whoever desires the Hereafter and strives for it with an en-*
> *deavour worthy of it, should he be faithful,—the endeavour*
> *of such will be well-appreciated. To these and to those—to*
> *all We extend the bounty of your Lord, and the bounty of*
> *your Lord is not confined. Observe how We have given some*
> *of them an advantage over some others; yet the Hereafter is*
> *surely greater in respect of ranks and greater in respect of*
> *relative merit.*[9]

The issues of being concerned with the hereafter and its details and knowing the worlds that the human will pass through and what obstacles and dangers await him is not to be considered an intellectual waste of time. Rather, it is a critical issue because like one strives to live a good life and works hard to accomplish that, he must also find the means and avenues to attain the good living in the eternal life. It is also imperative to understand the dangers and obstacles that surround his journey and the means to protect against these dangers after this life. It is noteworthy to mention that a person's life in this world and the nature of his behavior and actions are what determine his status in the next life and the nature of the life he lives there. Additionally, the real effects of his actions in this life will manifest themselves in the next life as either the presence of obstacles and dangers or the absence of obstacles and dangers. The noble narrations em-

---

[9] The Holy Quran. Chapter 17 [The Ascension; Arabic: *Al-Israa*]. Verse 18-21.

phasize that there is a long travel that we must complete to attain the eternal life. The Commander of the Faithful states, *"Woe because of [having so] little provisions, the long road [ahead], the distant travel, and the gravity of the destination..."*[10]

The narrations further emphasize the amount of hurdles that one will encounter which amounts to, as Al-Sadouq Muhammad Ibn Babouyah (May God bless his soul) narrates on behalf of Abi Abd God Al-Sadik (a), *"Between this life and the hereafter are one thousand obstacles, the easiest is death."*[11]

The Scholars of Islam emphasized the stages and worlds that a person passes through on his journey to the eternal life, the real life that the Holy Quran describes as being plentiful. This real life that is filled with energy and activity is after death. The reason why scholars directed great attention to this subject is because there is an abundance of narrations that speak about these afterworlds. Amongst those that have written on this subject is the revered scholar, Sayyid Hashem Al-Bahrani. He wrote a detailed book titled "Ma'lim Al-Zulfa". We also find a summarized book, to a certain extent, which is "Manazil Al-Akhira" written by Al-Shaikh Abbas Alqumi (May God bless his soul) and a treatise written by Alama Al-Tabatabaei titled "Hayat Ma Bad Al-Mawt". In addition, there are other books that focus on life after death, which I find are extremely important to read. Moreover, we should attempt to follow what is prescribed in these valuable books, which derive from the Holy Quran and the purified tradition in addressing many of the problems that humans might encounter after this world.

[10] Al-Majlisi, *Bihar Al-Anwar*, 70:128.
[11] Al-Sadouq, *Man La Yahtharahu Al-Faqih*, 1:124.

In this summarized lesson, we will shed light on some of the levels, or as the Ethic Scholars refer to as the stages, which are stations that a person must pass by before arriving at the final destination. That final destination is one that he has decided for himself through his actions and deeds in this world. These stages describe what fear and obstacles he will face, and each stage's role in purifying him from the effects of sins. That way, if he was from the faithful and on the path of excellence, he can reach eternal happiness. However, if he was from the evildoers, the fears and obstacles are only a slight taste of the punishment that God has prepared for the sinful as a result of his deeds.

> The Book will be set up. Then you will see the guilty apprehensive of what is in it. They will say, 'Woe to us! What a book is this! It omits nothing, big or small, without enumerating it.' They will find present whatever they had done, and your Lord does not wrong anyone. [12]

God also says,

> The day when every soul will find present whatever good it has done; and as for the evil, it has done, it will wish there were a far distance between it and itself. God warns you to beware of [disobeying] Him, and God is most kind to [His] servants. [13]

We will attempt to refer to the effects of the worldly deeds in creating the hardships and struggles or in eliminating them so that one does not encounter them in his journey to the eternal life. The most important stage is death.

---

[12] The Holy Quran. Chapter 18 [The Cave; Arabic: *Al-Kahf*]. Verse 49.
[13] The Holy Quran. Chapter 3 [Arabic: *Aal Imran*]. Verse 30.

One of the realities that is not doubted is death, which God has ordained on his creation. God states in the Holy Quran, *"There is a [preordained] time for every nation: when their time comes, they shall not defer it by a single hour nor shall they advance it."*[14] This is the breaking point between this world and what comes after it. Thus, it is the last stage of this life and the first stage of the hereafter. The death process differs, in its harshness and easiness, from one person to another. Some experience a very easy process that is pain free while others face extreme pain and fear. Here we must reference the hardships that a person might encounter during this process in addition to the relaxation that a believer might experience. Amongst the struggles during death are the following.

PREVIEW AND EXPOSURE OF THE TRUTH

Man lives in this world and does not observe except the appearance of things and that which he can sense with his five senses. This only represents the modicum of what actually surrounds the human. For he does not see the effects of the deeds he performs let alone the metaphysical environment around him. That is despite the fact that it manifests and is connected to the person. If it is positive, it results in security, tranquility and a good life. If it is negative, it can cause struggle and wretchedness of life. Nonetheless, one cannot observe these things because he is generally not able to sense anything except that which the five senses pick up. Moreover, it is impossible to physically view the metaphysical worlds. However, as soon as he enters the state of death, the realities start to reveal themselves and he is able to

---

[14] The Holy Quran. Chapter 7 [The Heights; Arabic: *Al-Araf*]. Verse 34.

somehow see the true impact of his deeds. If those deeds
are righteous ones, they manifest to him in the best of
forms and if they are bad, they will show up in the worse
and ugliest of forms. This is what the narrations explain.
Here, the barriers are removed and the human observes the
reality of things as the Holy Quran describes, *"You were certainly oblivious of this. We have removed your veil from you, and so
today your eyesight is acute."*[15]

Is there any scene more frightening than when a person observes his actions manifest to be among the ugliest of creatures and having the worst of stenches? The ugliness and
the stench reveals the true nature of one's evil deeds. These
accompany one to his grave and resurrection, until one is
presented before God.

THE ANGEL OF DEATH

There is no doubt that a human lives a state of fear and
panic and when encountering the angel of death because
this generous angel treats the sinful and obedient believers
differently. He appears to the sinful in the ugliest of forms.
Some of the narrations describe him to be, *"A black man
with his hair standing up, a bad stench, and black clothes. Smoke and
flames of fire drips from his mouth and nostrils."*[16]

However, he appears to the obedient believers in the most
beautiful of forms conveying to them glad tidings of heaven
and bringing tranquility and joy to their hearts such that
they do not feel any fear or terror.

---

[15] The Holy Quran. Chapter 50 [Arabic: *Qaf*]. Verse 22.
[16] Al-Majlisi, *Bihar Al-Anwar*, 6:143.

THE PROPHET AND AHLULBAYT

One of the things that the Followers of Ahlulbayt (a) believe in is the presence of the Prophet (p), the Commander of the Faithful (a), Lady Fatima (a), Imam Hasan (a) and Imam Husain (a) at every person's death. This is mentioned by numerous authentic narrations and thus, is widely accepted by the Followers of Ahlulbayt (a). One of the narrations is related by Al-Harith Al-Hamdani (May God be pleased with him),

> *I went to the Commander of the Faithful (a). He said,* 'what brought you?' *I replied,* '*my love for you oh Commander of the Faithful (a).*' *He told me,* 'oh Harith, do you love me?' *I answered,* '*by God yes oh Commander of the Faithful (a).*' *He said,* 'when your soul reaches your throat [during death], you will find me where you desire...'[17]

It is important to mention that some doubt this issue and question how the Immaculates can attend more than one person's death simultaneously. In answering this question, there are two points;

First: The laws that govern the materialistic world are different than the laws of the world beyond. What is impossible in the materialistic world can be possible in the world beyond because the governing laws and rules are different.

Second: Like the angel of death comes to every person during death no matter how many deaths are happening simultaneously, this is also possible with the Prophet (p) and

---

[17] Ibid, 6:181.

Ahlulbayt (a) who are undoubtedly better and of a higher status than the angel of death. Nonetheless, observing and feeling the presence of the Prophet (p) and Ahlulbayt (a) is different from one believer to another. It is narrated on the behalf of Imam Al-Ridha (a) on the behalf of his forefathers (a), "*Imam Ali Ibn Abi Taleb (a) stated, whoever loves me will find me at his death in the way he is pleased. And whoever hates me will find me at his death in the way he is displeased.*"[18]

The narrations emphasized on this meaning. The believer does not experience except that which he loves from them, may God send his blessings on them. Abu Baseer narrates the following from Imam Sadiq (a):

> *If a person is in the state of death [on his deathbed] such that he is not able to speak, the Prophet (p) and whoever God wills come to him. The Prophet (p) would sit to his right and the other would sit to his left. The Prophet (p) would inform him that which you desired is before you and that which you feared you are protected from. Then a door to paradise opens to him. The Prophet (p) tells him, this is your place in paradise...*[19]

The disbelievers will not see from them except that which is disliked. Ibn Abi Yafour narrates,

> *Khaṭṭab Al-Juhani was one of our acquaintances and he was extreme in his hatred to the Household of Muhammed (p)... So I entered [his place to visit] as a [social gesture] and out of dissimulation. I found him unconscious, facing the moments of death. Then I heard him say, 'what is be-*

---

[18] Ibid, 6:188
[19] Ibid, 6:196

tween us oh Ali.' I informed Aba Abd Allah (p) of this and he said, 'I swear by the Lord of the Kaaba, he saw him. I swear by the Lord of the Kaaba, he saw him. I swear by the Lord of the Kaaba, he saw him.*[20]*

When one of us attempts to imagine this scenario and how difficult it can be where the disobedient sinner sees the angel of death in the most terrifying of forms, finds the people he is dependent on inattentive to him, and observes his deeds manifest as ugly beings, one cannot help but be in a state of fear. One may be terrified and may panic during such moments in which he is in most need of calmness, tranquility, and security. As for the believers who were righteous, to them are glad tidings. In those moments, they only experience joy, rest, and security.

THE DEPARTING OF THE SOUL

One of the major struggles that one faces during death is the departing of the soul and the throes of death. As is narrated on behalf of Imam Sadiq (a),

The Commander of the Faithful (a) ailed of [an illness to] his eye, so the Prophet (s) visited him and heard him shouting. The Prophet (s) said, 'is this out of despair or pain?' [Imam Ali (a)] said, 'oh Messenger of God, I have never felt a pain harsher than this.' [The Prophet (s) said, 'oh Ali! When the angel of death descends to reap the soul of a disbeliever, he would come with a skewer of fire that he uses to take the soul. At that moment, hellfire [itself] would

---

[20] Ibid, 6:200

shout.'[Imam] Ali (a) sat up straight and said, 'oh Messenger of God (s), repeat to me your words, as what you have said has made me forget my pain.' [Imam Ali (a)] then said, 'Will this befall anyone from your nation?' [The Prophet (s)] said, 'Yes. An oppressive governor, anyone who takes the wealth of the orphans unjustly, and the dishonest witness.[21]

The departing of the soul is one of the greatest pains that we will come across. We see that when one of us loses breath he feels a severe pain and discomfort. How then can we bear the pain of the departure of the soul?

However, there are a number of narrations that tell us that the soul of the believers will depart their bodies painlessly. It is narrated that Imam Askari (a) said,

[Imam] Sadiq (a) was asked to describe death. He (a) said, 'To the believer, it will be like the most fragrant of aromas. He will smell it and become drowsy because of the fragrance. All fatigue and pain would be cut off from him. For the disbeliever, it will be like the bites of snakes and the stings of scorpions, or even worse.' It was said [by someone present], 'some say that it is harsher than the thrusts of saws, the gnawing of shears, the breaking of bones, and the grinding of the millstones on the pupils [of the eyes]. [Imam Sadiq (a)] said, 'it is like that for some of the disbelievers and the dissolute....[22]

---

[21] Ibid, 6:170. Citing, Al-Kulayni, Al-Kafi, 3:253-254.
[22] Ibid, 6:152.

The Quran describes the difference between the afterlife of a believer and the afterlife of a disbeliever. As for the believer,

> *Look! The friends of God will indeed have no fear nor will they grieve – those who have faith and are God-wary. For them is good news in the life of this world and in the Hereafter. (There is no altering the words of God.) That is the great success.*[23]

On the other hand, the Quran describes the afterlife of the disbeliever in the verse,

> *Were you to see when the angels take away the faithless, striking their faces and their backs, [saying], 'Taste the punishment of the burning. That is because of what your hands have sent ahead, and because God is not tyrannical to the servants.*[24]

This doesn't mean that no believer will ever taste the harsh pains of the departure of the soul. Rather, some believers may still suffer through this pain during death so that the pain sheds away any misdeeds that they may have committed in their life and so they can reach greater proximity to God. A number of narrations have emphasized this, including the hadith of Imam Sadiq (a) where he says, *"The Messenger of God (s) said, '[the pain of] death is an atonement for the sins of a believer.'"*[25]

Al-Mufaddal also narrates that Imam Sadiq (a) said,

---

[23] The Holy Quran. Chapter 10 [Arabic: *Yunus*]. Verse 62-64.

[24] The Holy Quran. Chapter 8 [Arabic: *Al-Anfaal*]. Verse 50-51.

[25] Al-Majlisi, *Bihar Al-Anwar*, 6:151. Citing, Al-Tusi, *Al-Amaali*, 110.

Oh Mufaddal, beware of sins and warn our followers. By God, [the repercussions of sins] do not reach anyone as quickly as they reach you. One of you may be harassed by a governor, and that would be caused by his own sins. He would be struck with illness, and that would be caused by his own sins. He would be stripped of some blessings, and that would be caused by his own sins. He would face harsh pains at death, and that would be caused by his own sins. [It would be] such that those around him would say that he has been overwhelmed by death. Do you know why this is so, Mufaddal? [...] It is, by God, so that you are not judged for them in the hereafter, as [their punishments] have been expedited for you in this world.[26]

Yet, this does not mean that we should feel safety from the punishment of the hereafter because we have seen the trials of this world. First of all, the severities of these trials, and especially the throes of death, are great enough for us to attempt to avoid them. Secondly, this may not be enough for you to avoid the punishment of the hereafter. Finally, the excess of sin can remove a person from being a believer to the status of disbeliever, God forbid. If that becomes the case, these pains will be the beginning of eternal punishment.

EASING THE THROES OF DEATH

Every reward or punishment that an individual faces, from the beginning of his journey to the final destination that is the hereafter, is dictated by the individual's choice-making.

---

[26] Al-Sadouq. *'Ilal al-Shara'i'*, 1:297.

It is all a consequence of the individual's free-willed actions. And because of the infinite nature of God's mercy, He has provided us with a number of means for easing the throes of death through actions that we can take before reaching that state. It will suffice us to mention here one example, as other examples can easily be found in books of ethics.

Our traditions tell us that one of the greatest effects we can have in easing the throes of death comes from our relationship with our parents. It is narrated that Imam Sadiq (a) said, "*whoever likes for God to ease on him the throes of death, let him connect with his kin and honor his parents. If an individual were so, God would ease on him the throes of death and he would not ever be inflicted with poverty.*"[27]

RENOUNCING FAITH AT DEATH

One of the greatest dangers that a person can face is renouncing faith at the time of death. Some people may, at the time of death, alter their faith and begin to disbelieve after having lived their lives as Muslims.

The Quran addresses this root of this phenomenon when it speaks of the place of faith in the heart as being either permanent or temporary – "*It is He who created you from a single soul, then there is the [enduring] abode and the place of temporary lodging. We have certainly elaborated the signs for a people who understand.*"[28]

The narrations of the Immaculate Imams (a) explain the meaning of this verse and that it is speaking of the place of

---

[27] Al-Majlisi, *Bihar Al-Anwar*, 71:66. Citing, Al-Sadouq, *Al-Amaali*, 318.

[28] The Holy Quran. Chapter 6 [The Cattle; Arabic: *Al-Anaam*]. Verse 98.

faith within an individual. Our Imams (a) tell us that faith may take a permanent position within the heart and minds of the true believers, but may also take a temporary position within the hearts of some. It is narrated that Imam Ridha (a) said,

> God has guided you and enlightened you. [Imam Sadiq (a)] used to say, 'surely, it is an enduring abode and a temporary lodging. The enduring abode is robust faith, and the temporary lodging is lent [temporary] faith.' Would you be able to guide whomever God has misguided?[29, 30]

Of course, whether faith takes hold in a person's heart or leaves it after a temporary visit is not decided arbitrarily by God – He is Exalted over this. Rather, these are consequences of the individual's actions and character. If a person has true conviction in his faith and acts according to it, it will never be stripped away from him. However, if a person has a shallow external level of belief, he may be stripped of the blessings and guidance that allowed him to maintain it. As the narration of Imam Sadiq (a) states, *"God is the All-Just. He has called His servants to belief in Him and not to disbelief in Him. Whomever believes in God and that belief is reaffirmed with God, God would not move him from faith to disbelief."*[31]

This narration evidences the fact that renouncing one's faith at death is only a consequence of the individual's actions. If a person believes and obeys the commands of God, he will be able to hold fast to his faith even during the great pains

---

[29] In the sense that such a person chose to deviate with the ability God gave him

[30] Al-Majlisi, *Bihar Al-Anwar*, 66:222.

[31] Ibid, 66:213.

of death. However, if a person claims to believe but in reality carries in him the seeds of deviance, hypocrisy, and disbelief, that will be a cause for him to renounce his faith, even if only at the moments of death. That is why the Commander of the Faithful (a) instructed us not to judge anyone by the faith they carried throughout their lives, but rather by the faith that they carried at the time of death. It is narrated that he said, *"of faith is that which is sturdy and stable in the hearts, and that which is lent between hearts and chests until a time known [by God]. If you are ever to disown anyone give him time until his death. It is then that the threshold for disowning is met."*[32]

Therefore, we must safeguard ourselves from this danger. This can be achieved through a number of steps.

Firstly, we must pay great importance to understanding our beliefs and implanting them deep within our hearts. Weakness of faith is one of the causes of renouncing faith at the time of death. *"Certain [Divine] precedents have passed before you. So travel through the land and observe how was the fate of the deniers."*[33]

God also said, *"Then the fate of those who committed misdeeds was that they denied the signs of God and they used to deride them."*[34]

The righteous of our honorable scholars and the companions of the Holy Household (a) have always given great weight to this issue. So we find Abd Al-Adheem Al-Hasani (r) – a Shia notable scholar, and a descendant of Imam Hasan ibn Ali ibn Abi Talib (a) – would seek Imam Ali Al-

[32] Al-Radi, *Nahjul Balagha*, 2:386, Sermon 189.

[33] The Holy Quran. Chapter 3 [Arabic: *Aal Imran*]. Verse 137.

[34] The Holy Quran. Chapter 30 [The Romans; Arabic: *Al-Room*]. Verse 10.

Hadi (a) to confirm with him his creed. He narrates the following:

> *I walked in on my master Ali ibn Muhammad [Al-Hadi]*
> *(a). When he saw me he said to me, 'Welcome, oh*
> *Abou Al-Qasim!*[35] *You are truly of our followers.'*
> *So I told him, 'Oh son of the Messenger of God (a), I*
> *would like to confirm my creed with you. If it is pleasing [to*
> *God], I will stand strong by it until I meet God, the Exalt-*
> *ed and Glorified.' [The Imam (a)] said, 'give it to me oh*
> *Abou Al-Qasim.*[36]

Al-Hasani (r) went on to list the core beliefs of Shia Muslims, and the Imam (a) confirmed them all. This indicates to us the importance of having a strong basis in theology to allow the faith to take root in the heart.

Secondly, we must do our best to avoid all sin and deviance, and work to live a life to ensure the best of outcomes in the hereafter. There are a number of deeds that ensure the best of outcomes for the individual, such as keeping good relations with kin, performing the daily prayers on time, helping those who are in need, having good manners, and paying the alms, among the many acts that ensure the best outcome for the person.

On the flip side, there are many actions that ensure the worst of outcomes for the individual. Those include disbelief in parts of the faith and its rituals, being excessive in sin, and others. In one narration, it is reported that Imam Ridha (a) said,

---

[35] Aboul Qasim was the *Kunya*, or nickname, of Abd Al-Adheem Al-Hasani (r).
[36] Al-Sadouq, *Ikmal al-Din*, 376.

[Imam] Al-Sadiq (a) wrote to some people that 'if you wish that [the last of your deeds] are the best of your deeds so that you [face death] while you have the best of deeds, then glorify God's rights by not using His blessings to disobey Him. Do not take for granted His patience over you. Honor whoever ... ascribes to our love....[37]

Thirdly, we must increase our mentioning of God and supplicating to Him. The Holy Household of the Prophet (s) have mentioned to us many supplications and means by which we can seek proximity to God and seek refuge in Him from this terrible fate. This includes:

1. The supplications specifically dealing with *'Adela*, or renouncing faith at death, which are mentioned in the books of supplications;
2. Persistence in performing the daily prayers on time;
3. Supplication with the verse: *"Our Lord! Do not make our hearts swerve after You have guided us, and bestow Your mercy on us. Indeed, You are the All-munificent."*[38]
4. Persistence in reciting the glorifications of Lady Zahraa (a).[39]

This is amongst other supplications and actions that can be performed. Persistence in these actions will grant the servant of God robust and everlasting faith, God-willing.

---

[37] Al-Sadouq, *'Uyoon Akhbar Al-Rida*, 2:7.

[38] The Holy Quran. Chapter 3 [Arabic: *Aal Imran*]. Verse 8.

[39] The glorifications of Lady Zahraa (a) are usually recited after prayers. They consist of reciting the following 3 glorifications: *"Allah Akbar"* 34 times, *"Alhamd li Allah"* 33 times, and *"Subhan Allah"* 33 times.

BIBLIOGRAPHY

RELIGIOUS SCRIPTURE

The Holy Quran

OTHER SOURCES

Al-Ameen, Muhsen. *Aa'yan Al-Shia*. 5th ed. Beirut: Daar Al-Taaruf.

Al-Amili, Muhammad ibn Al-Hassan. *Wasael Al-Shia*. Beirut: Daar Ihya Al-Torath Al-Arabi.

Al-Barqi, Ahmad ibn Muhammad. *Al-Mahasin*. Tehran: Daar Al-Kutub Al-Islamiya, 1950.

Al-Beshwaei, Mahdi. *Sirat al-A'immah*. Muasasat Al-Imam Al-Sadiq.

Al-Borojourdi, Agha Hussein. *Jami' Ahadeeth Al-Shia*. Qum: Al-Matba'a Al-Ilmiyya, 1978.

Al-Bukhari, Muhammad ibn Ismael. *Sahih Bukhari*. Beirut: Daar Al-Fikr, 1981.

Al-Harrani, Al-Hassan ibn Ali. *Tohaf Al-'Oqool*. Qum: Muasasat Al-Nashr Al-Islami, 1983.

Al-Haydari, Kamal. *Al-Tawheed*. Daar Al-Sadiqayn, 1992.

Al-Ḥaydari, Kamal. *Buḥuth ḥawl al-Imamah*. Beirut, Muasasat al-Imam Al-Jawad, 2013.

Al-Hilli, Al-Hassan ibn Yusuf. *Kashf Al-Murad fe Sharh Tajreed Al-I'tiqad*. Qum: Muasasat Al-Nashr Al-Islami, 1996.

Al-Hindi, Ali Al-Muttaqi. *Kanz Al-'Amal*. Muasasat Al-Risala, 1989.

Al-Jaafari, Muhammad Rida. *Al-Ghayba*. Qum: Markaz Al-Abhath Al-Aqaediya, 1999.

Al-Lari, Mujtaba. *Dirasa fi Usus Al-Islam*. Translated by Kamal Al-Sayyid.

Al-Majlisi, Muhammad Baqir. *Bihar Al-Anwar*. Beirut: Al-Wafaa, 1983.

Al-Majlisi, Muhammad Baqir. *Mir'at al-'uqul fi Sharh Akhbar 'al al-Rasul*. Tehran: Daar Al-Kutub Al-Islamiya, 1983.

Al-Mufid, Muhammad ibn Muhammad. *Al-Irshad*. Beirut: Daar Al-Mufeed, 1993.

Al-Muqarram, Abdulrazzaq Al-Mousawi. *Maqtal Al-Hussain (a)*. Qum: Daar Al-Thaqafa li Al-Tiba'a wa Al-Nashr, 1990.

Al-Mutahhari, Murtada. *Al-'Adl Al-Ilahi*. Beirut: Al-Daar Al-Islamiya, 1985.

Al-Mutahhari, Murtada. *Al-Islam wa Mutatalibat al-Asr*. Mashhad: Majma Al-Buhooth Al-Islamiya, 1990.

Al-Nisabouri, Abu Abdullah Al-Hakim. *Al-Mustadrak*. Beirut: Daar Al-Marifa.

Al-Nouri, Mirza Hussain. *Mustadrak Al-Wasa'el*. Beirut: Mu'asasat Aal Al-Bayt li Ihya' Al-Torath.

Al-Qandouzi, Suleiman ibn Ibrahim. *Yanabee' Al-Mawadda*. Daar Al-Oswa, 1995.

Al-Qummi, Ali ibn Muhammad Al-Khazzaz. *Kifayet Al-Athar*. Qum: Al-Khayyam, 1980.

Al-Radi, Muhammad ibn Al-Hussain. *Nahj Al-Balagha*. Beirut: Daar Al-Ma'rifa.

Al-Rawandi, Fadlallah ibn Ali. *Al-Nawadir*. Qum: Daar Al-Hadeeth, 1998.

Al-Rawandi, Saeed ibn Hibatallah. *Al-Kharayij*. Qum: Muasasat Al-Imam Al-Mahdi.

Al-Reyshahri, Muhammad. *Mizan Al-Hikma*. Cairo: Daar Al-Hadith, 1995.

Al-Sadouq, Muhammad ibn Ali. *'Ilel Al-Sharai'*. Najaf: Al-Matbaa Al-Haydaria, 1966.

Al-Sadouq, Muhammad ibn Ali. *'Uyoon Akhbar Al-Rida*. Beirut: Al-A'lami, 1984.

Al-Sadouq, Muhammad ibn Ali. *Al-'Itiqadat fee deen Al-Imamiyya*. Beirut: Daar Al-Mufid, 1993.

Al-Sadouq, Muhammad ibn Ali. *Al-Amaali*. Qum: Muassasat Al-Bitha, 1996.

Al-Sadouq, Muhammad ibn Ali. *Al-Khisal*. Qum: Jama'at Al-Mudarriseen, 1982.

Al-Sadouq, Muhammad ibn Ali. *Ikmal al-Din*. Qum: Muasasat Al-Nashr Al-Islami, 1984.

Al-Sadouq, Muhammad ibn Ali. *Ma'ani Al-Akhbar*. Qum: Muasasat Al-Nashr Al-Islami, 1942.

Al-Sadouq, Muhammad ibn Ali. *Man La Yahtharahu Al-Faqih*. 2nd ed. Qum: Jama'at Al-Mudarriseen.

Al-Sadouq, Muhammad ibn Ali. *Thawab Al-'Amal*. Qum: Muassasat Al-Bitha, 1989.

Al-Sadr, Muhammad. *Tareekh Al-Ghayba Al-Kubra*. Beirut: Daar Al-Taaruf, 1992.

Al-Saffar, Muhammad ibn Al-Hassan. *Basa'er Al-Darajat*. Tehran: Al-A'lami, 1983.

Al-Samhudi, Ali ibn Abdullah. *Wafaa' Al-Wafa bi Akhbar Daar Al-Mustafa*. Beirut: Daar Ihya Al-Torath Al-Arabi.

Al-Shirazi, Nasir Makarim. *Al-Amthal*. Madrasat Ameer Al-Mumineen.

Al-Subḥani, Jaafar. *Al-'aqsam fi al-Qur'an al-Karim*.

Al-Subhani, Jaafar. *Fe Thilal Al-Tawheed*. Qum: Muasasat Al-Imam Al-Sadiq, 1991.

Al-Tabatabaei, Muhammad Hussain. *Tafsir Al-Mizan*. Qum: Jama'at Al-Mudarriseen.

Al-Tabrasi, Ahmad ibn Ali. *Al-Ihtijaj*. Najaf: Al-Nu'man, 1966.

Al-Tabrasi, Ameen Al-Deen. *Mujamma' Al-Bayan*. Beirut: Al-A'lami, 1995.

Al-Tusi, Muhammad ibn Al-Hassan. *Al-Amaali*. Qum, 1993.

Al-Tusi, Muhammad ibn Al-Hassan. *Al-Ghayba*. Qum: Muasasat Al-Maarif Al-Islamiya, 1990.

Al-Tusi, Muhammad ibn Al-Hassan. *Al-Tahtheeb*. Tehran: Daar Al-Kutub Al-Islamiya, 1970.

Al-Tusi, Muhammad ibn Al-Hassan. *Al-Tibyan*. Daar Ihya Al-Torath Al-Arabi, 1988.

Al-Tusi, Muhammad ibn Al-Hassan. *Ikhtiyar Ma'rifat Al-Rijaal*. Qum: Muasasat Aal Al-Bayt, 1983.

Al-Tusi, Muhammad ibn Al-Hassan. *Misbah Al-Mutahajjid*. Beirut: Fiqh Al-Shia, 1991.

Al-Wasiti, Kafi Al-Deen Al-Laithi. *'Uyoon Al-Hikam wa Al-Mawa'ez*. Qum: Daar Al-Hadith.

Al-Yazdi, Muhammad Taqi Misbah. *Al-Manhaj Al-Jadeed fe Ta'leem Al-Falsafa*. Muasasat Al-Nadhr Al-Islamiya, 1989.

Al-Zamkhashri, Mahmoud ibn Omar. *Tafseer Al-Kashaf*. Egypt, 1966.

Dah'lan, Ahmad ibn Zayni. *Al-Durrar Al-Saniyya*. Istanbul: Eishiq, 1976.

Ibn Hanbal, Ahmad. *Musnad Ahmad*. Beirut: Daar Saadir.

Ibn Qawlaweih, Jaafar ibn Muhammad. *Kaamil Al-Ziyarat*. Qum: Muasasat Al-Nashr Al-Islami, 1996.

Ibn Shahrashoob, Muhammad ibn Ali. *Al-Manaqib*. Najaf: Al-Matbaa Al-Haydaria, 1956.

Ibn Tawuus, Ali ibn Moussa. *Iqbaal Al-A'mal*. Qum: Maktab Al-Ilam Al-Islami, 1993.

Rufai'i, Jaafar. *Tazkiyat An-Nafs wa Tahtheeb Al-Rooh*. Daar Al-Hadi, 2001.